RUN TO DAYLIGHT!

RUN TO DAYLIGHT!

By
VINCE LOMBARDI
with W. C. HEINZ

TEMPO
BOOKS

GROSSET & DUNLAP
New York

ISBN: 0-448-05392-6

TEMPO BOOKS EDITION, 1968
BY ARRANGEMENT WITH PRENTICE-HALL, INC.
FIRST PRINTING, AUGUST 1968
SECOND PRINTING, OCTOBER 1968
THIRD PRINTING, FEBRUARY 1969
FOURTH PRINTING, JUNE 1969
FIFTH PRINTING, APRIL 1971

To Marie, Susan, Vincent, my assistant
coaches and the Green Bay Packers Football Team and to all of those who make
professional football a great game.

PRINTED IN THE UNITED STATES OF AMERICA

FOREWORD

The small room where this is written is lined with books on sports. Some are a joy to read. Some are valuable as reference works. Some are proof that the English language can be a gun the author didn't know was loaded.

Except for the fact that all of them concern sports—barring the dictionary, the thesaurus, the Bible and Bartlett's *Familiar Quotations*—none of the books around me has much in common with the book before me. This is an original, the product of what we hope is an original concept.

We said, "Let's try something new. Let us get the top authority in each game to say what he has to say about his game. Let us get the finest writer in the field to collaborate with this man, and the finest artist in the field to illustrate their work. If this doesn't produce the best book in the field, let us all retire to bee-keeping."

How do you pack into a single book what Vince Lombardi feels about football, what he knows of the game, how he thinks of the people around him, what he remembers of his beginnings in the sport? Bill Heinz chose to compress it into one typical week of a typical season. It turned out to be a crucial week in a big season, but that was a mere happen-so.

In the world of Vince Lombardi, any week in any season is as big as any other week in any other season. That's why Bill Heinz wanted to call this book "Six Days and Sunday." He was dissuaded by the sure knowledge that it would wind up among Biblical tracts on the booksellers' shelves.

After this book was written, Paul Hornung of the Packers and Alex Karras of the Lions were suspended for betting on games and five Detroit colleagues of Karras were fined. This did not alter anything Vince Lombardi had to say about those men, and not a line was changed.

Red Smith

AUTHORS' NOTE

In the pages that follow we have attempted to record as accurately as possible the preparations for and the playing of a Green Bay Packers game of the 1962 season. Although this book is concerned with a specific game, it has been our hope to present the seven days involved in such a way that the reader, no matter to what team he devotes his allegiance, may better understand what his own, or any team, experiences each week of the season. For that reason the Packers' opponent, who will undoubtedly be identified by professional football followers, remains unidentified here. Throughout the text the reader will find many references to offensive and defensive formations, pass routes and patterns and key plays. Therefore an appendix in which these are diagrammed has been provided.

Vince Lombardi

W. C. Heinz

MONDAY

3:15 A.M.

I have been asleep for three hours and, suddenly, I am awake. I am wide awake, and that's the trouble with this game. Just twelve hours ago I walked off that field, and we had beaten the Bears 49 to 0. Now I should be sleeping the satisfied sleep of the contented but I am lying here awake, wide awake, seeing myself walking across that field, seeing myself searching in the crowd for George Halas but really hoping that I would not find him.

All week long there builds up inside of you a competitive animosity toward that other man, that counterpart across the field. All week long he is the symbol, the epitome, of what you must defeat and then, when it is over, when you have looked up to that man for as long as I have looked up to George Halas, you cannot help but be disturbed by a score like this. You know he brought a team in here hurt by key injuries and that this was just one of those days, but you can't apologize. You can't apologize for a score. It is up there on that board and nothing can change it now. I can just hope, lying here awake in the middle of the night, that after all those years he has had in this league—and he has had forty-two of them—these things no longer affect him as they still affect me. I can just hope that I am making more of this than he is, and now I see myself, unable to find him in the crowd and walking up that ramp and into our dressing room, now searching instead for something that will bring my own team back to earth.

"All right!" I said. "Let me have your attention. That was a good effort, a fine effort. That's the way to play this game, but remember this. You beat the Bears, but you know as well

7

as I do that they weren't ready. They had key personnel hurt and they weren't up for this game. Those people who are coming in here next week will be up. They won again today, so they're just as undefeated as we are. They'll be coming in here to knock your teeth down your throats, so remember that. Have your fun tonight and tomorrow, but remember that."

"Right, coach!" someone behind me, maybe Fuzzy Thurston or Jerry Kramer or Ray Nitschke, shouted. "Way to talk, coach!"

Am I right and is that the way to talk, or has this become a game for madmen and am I one of them? Any day that you score seven touchdowns in this league and turn in a shutout should be a day of celebration. Even when the Bears are without Bill George, who is the key to their defense, and Willie Galimore, who is their speed, this is a major accomplishment. But where is the elation?

Once there was elation. In 1959, in the first game I ever coached here, that I ever head-coached anywhere in pro ball, we beat these Bears 9 to 6 and I can remember it clearly. I can remember them leading us into the last period and then Jimmy Taylor going in from the 5 on our 28-Weak, and Paul Hornung kicking the point, and then Hank Jordan breaking through on the blitz and nailing Ed Brown in the end zone for the safety. The year before, this team had won only one game and tied one out of twelve, so now they were carrying me off the field because a single league victory was once cause enough for celebration.

What success does to you. It is like a habit-forming drug that, in victory, saps your elation and, in defeat, deepens your despair. Once you have sampled it you are hooked, and now I lie in bed, not sleeping the sleep of the victor but wide awake, seeing the other people who are coming in next Sunday with the best defensive line in the league, with that great middle linebacker, that left defensive halfback who is as quick and agile as a cat and a quarterback who, although he is not as daring as Johnny Unitas or Y. A. Tittle or Bobby Layne, can kill you with his consistency.

I don't see them as I do from the sideline, but as I have seen them over and over in the films. I see them beating us 17-13 in our opener in Milwaukee in 1961. I see them beating us 23-10 in their own park the year before, and that's what I mean about success. My mind does not dwell on the two games we beat them in 1959 or the single games we took from them in 1960 and again in 1961. For the most part you

8

remember only your losses, and it reminds me again of Earl Blaik and West Point after Navy beat our undefeated Army team 14-2 in 1950.

"All right," the Colonel would say whenever there was a lull. "Let's get out that Navy film."

You could see the other coaches sneak looks at one another, and although you couldn't hear the groans you could feel them in the room. Then we'd all file out and into the projection room once more.

"Look at that," the Colonel would say. "The fullback missed the block on that end."

How many times we had seen that fullback miss that block on that end I do not know. I do know that every time we saw that film Navy beat Army again, 14-2, and that was one of the ways Earl Blaik, the greatest coach I have ever known, paid for what he was.

So what I see now is that opener in '61, the last time they beat us. I see them stopping us twice inside their 5-yard line. I see us running their quarterback out of his pocket, the rhythm of that pass play broken, and both their split end and Jesse Whittenton relax. I see that end start up and Whittenton slip and that end catch it and run it to the 1, and on the next play their fullback takes it in. Then I see them on our 13-yard line and their fullback misses his block and falls. As he gets up, their quarterback, in desperation, flips the ball to him and he walks the 13 yards for the score.

Lying there like this, in the stillness of my house and conscious of any sound and every sensation, I am aware now of the soreness of my gums. It is this way every Monday, because for those two hours on the sideline every Sunday I have been grinding my teeth, and when I get up at eight o'clock and put in my bridge I'll be aware of it again. That, come to think of it, is only fitting and proper, because that bridge had its beginnings in the St. Mary's game my junior year at Fordham. Early in that game I must have caught an elbow or forearm or fist, because I remember sitting in that Polo Grounds dressing room during halftime and it felt like every tooth in my head was loose.

8:40 A.M.

"So I judge you won't be home for dinner," Marie says, while I am having my second cup of coffee.

9

"No," I say, and that is another part of the price that you and your family must pay. Maybe I'm wrong, but the only way I know how to coach this game is all the way, and what it costs, Marie once explained.

"From Monday until Wednesday night," she said, "we don't talk to him. On Wednesday he has to go out there and convince himself and five other coaches and thirty-six football players."

8:50 A.M.

I drive down our street to the corner, and I have to wait there because at this hour the traffic is heavy going into town. It is heavy with men who must convince other men that they need more insurance or new storm windows or a new car or who must solve a heat-conduction problem or an efficiency lag, and there is not much difference between us. Some of us will do our jobs well and some will not, but we will all be judged by only one thing—the result.

"That's where I can't see that it means much," Vincent, Jr., said one evening last summer just before we went into training camp. Marie and our Susan were at the Fond Du Lac horse show, where Susan was showing her mahogany mare, and Vincent and I were eating out.

"I don't know what you're talking about," I said.

"You're always saying," Vincent said, "that the only way to play the game or do the job is the way you're convinced is right for you."

"That's correct," I said. "The rest will follow, or it won't."

"Then I can't see where there's much difference between winning or losing," Vincent said, "as long as you've done your job."

"There isn't much difference," I said, "except economic. You know that scoreboard doesn't begin to tell the story, but what goes up there controls your economic future and your prestige."

"They can keep the prestige," Vincent said.

He was twenty years old last summer, and I know what he meant. He was seventeen when we moved here from the East and he had no vote in our move, nor had Susan. He was 5 feet 10 and weighed 180 and had been an all-conference full-back in New Jersey, but one of the Wisconsin papers listed him as 6 feet 2, 210 and all-state, and another carried that ridiculous story that he was being offered cars to pick between the four high schools.

"I'll never forget that first day out here," he has said since. "There are a thousand kids in that school, and the first time I walked into that cafeteria a thousand heads turned and a thousand kids looked at me."

One afternoon Marie drove out to watch Vincent practice. While she was sitting in her car another car drove up and one of the kids in it shouted to someone on the sidelines.

"Which one is Lombardi?" he shouted, and Marie said she thought: Oh, please. Please leave him alone! He's just a seventeen-year-old boy. Please get off his back.

It must have been just about then that Marie came off the phone one evening. Someone had wanted her to do something and she had turned it down.

"Sometimes they claw at you," she said. "Just because your husband knows how to coach football they claw at you."

And Vincent looked up from that book he was reading and said, "Join the crowd, Mom."

8:52 A.M.

I'm in the line of traffic now, and I guess what it comes down to is that success demands singleness of purpose. In this game we're always looking for catch-phrases, especially with a connotation of masculinity, so I call it mental toughness. They have written about the mental toughness with which I supposedly have instilled this team and, when they ask me what it is, I have difficulty explaining it. I think it is singleness of purpose and, once you have agreed upon the price that you and your family must pay for success, it enables you to forget that price. It enables you to ignore the minor hurts, the opponent's pressure and the temporary failures, and I remember my first year here. I remember that first day of full practice in training camp, and when I walked back to the dressing room I wanted to cry. The lackadaisical ineptitude, almost passive resistance, was like an insidious disease that had infected almost a whole squad. The next morning, when I walked into the trainer's room, there must have been fifteen or twenty of them waiting for the whirlpool bath or the diathermy or for rubdowns.

"What is this?" I said. "An emergency casualty ward? Now get this straight. When you're hurt you have every right

11

to be in here. When you're hurt you'll get the best medical attention we can provide. We've got too much money invested in you to think otherwise, but this has got to stop. This is disgraceful. I have no patience with the small hurts that are bothering most of you. You're going to have to learn to live with small hurts and play with small hurts if you're going to play for me. Now I don't want to see anything like this again."

Then I walked out. The next day when I walked into that room there weren't fifteen or twenty in there. There were two, so maybe that's how you do it.

8:56 A.M.

There is a traffic light at the corner of Monroe and Mason and I stop behind a line of cars in the left lane. When that left-turn arrow turns green, and if everyone moves promptly, six cars can make that turn. Six days a week this traffic light is the one thing that invades my consciousness as I drive to work, that consistently interrupts that single purpose of winning next Sunday's game.

I tried to plant that seed of single purpose in the first squad letter I wrote before training camp that first year. I must have rewritten it ten or twelve times, trying to tell them what I hoped to do and how I hoped to do it without making it sound like I was setting up a slave-labor camp.

That summer, as every summer, the first-year men, which is what I call the rookies because I think it implies more respect, came into camp at St. Norbert College, just up the Fox River from here. They arrived three days before the veterans were due, but a half dozen of the veterans came with them. Then two of these veterans, two of my stars, took off on a frolic and I didn't see them again until I collared them in the hall on the third day.

"What do you think we're running here?" I hollered at them. "Just a home base where you can pick up your mail between social engagements? When you came into this camp, no matter how early, it was expected that you came here to work. . . ."

I've got all the emotions in excess and a hair-trigger controls them. I anger and I laugh and I cry quickly, and so I couldn't have told you five minutes later what else I said or just what I did. I have heard it told that I had one of them by his lapels and that it looked like I was going to bang his

head against the wall. They say you could
Sensenbrenner Hall, and that after it was ove
them walked into somebody's room and one of the
"I'm not gonna play for this — —. He's a madman."

An hour later I was leaving the dormitory to walk across
the campus to the science building for the first full-squad
meeting. They say I caught up with one of the two and
slapped him on the back and said, "C'mon, let's go to that
meeting." It's possible, because as fast as I heat up I cool off.

"And there's nothing personal about any of this," I was
telling them all a few minutes later. "Any criticism I make of
anyone, I make only because he's a ballplayer not playing
up to his potential. Any fine I levy on anyone, I levy because
he's hurting not only himself but thirty-five other men."

They were big men wedged into those varnished oak class-
room chairs with the writing arms on the right. They were
wearing shorts and slacks and short-sleeved sports shirts, and
I went into the regulations and my system of fines because
big as they are, sports-page heroes though they may be,
there is an almost adolescent impulsiveness in many of them.

This is something that the abandon with which football
must be played encourages. Beyond that, and for as long as
most of them can remember, which would be back to their
first days in grade school, they have been subject to regula-
tion. As their athletic ability turned them into privileged
high school and college celebrities, many of them became
masters at the art of circumvention.

I remember the two at the Giant camp at Winooski, Ver-
mont, who climbed the fire escape after curfew but picked
the wrong window and became entangled in the venetian
blinds in the room of Doc Sweeny, the Giant trainer. I remember the defensive end who was tiptoeing down the hall
one night, his shoes in his hand, when Jim Lee Howell, who
was coaching the Giants then, surprised him.

"You going somewhere?" Jim said.

"Why, yes," the end said, and you had to grade him high
on his speed of reaction. "I lost my wallet, so I thought I'd
go out and try to find it."

"I see," Jim said, looking at the shoes. "You planning to
sneak up on it?"

So in that first meeting I gave them the camp curfew: in
bed and lights out by eleven o'clock, midnight on Saturdays.
Any breaking of that curfew would cost the player $500.
Any player late for a meeting or practice would be fined $10
a minute, and any of them caught standing at a bar would

13

$150. Then I took a little off it by telling
point an Executive Committee, empowered to dis-
y fines or any grievances with me, and I said that all
ney collected would go into a team fund. With it the team
could throw a party, at a proper time, or put it to any other
use that they preferred, with the restriction that none of it
was to be returned to any fined player.

"Now I've already told you," I said, "the names of the
places that are off-limits in town. When we travel you'll be
given the names of all off-limits spots in every city. If you're
found in one of those places you won't be fined. You'll be off
the ball club."

I was reaching them where I knew I could hurt them—
in their pocketbooks—but a week later I caught the first one.
I hit him for $500, and when the Executive Committee came
to me, protesting that it was too stiff, I told them that if we
didn't set an example none of our regulations would be worth
anything, and I told them to talk it over again.

"We've talked it over," they said when they came back,
"and we agree the fine should stand."

But the game goes on. I would be naive to believe that w
can keep every one of thirty-six healthy, adventuresome males
confined for eight weeks with only an hour and a half off
six days a week and five hours off on Saturdays. Every year
there are three or four who try me, and every year there are
three or four who get knicked, and I can tell you before-
hand who they'll be and just about when they'll make their
tries.

So our five coaches and our personnel director pair off and
stand the watches. The first week of camp the heroes are
muscle sore and body weary, but a half hour after curfew
on the second Saturday one of them walks down the hall
from his room and stands in the open doorway of the office.
He is wearing undershorts and shower clogs and he waits,
like a small boy, for the coaches to look up.

"You want something?" one of them says.

"Yes," he says. "May I get a drink of water?"

"Why not?" the coach says.

"Thank you," he says.

They listen to the sound of the shower clogs on the hard
floor of the hall. They hear the clink of the coin in the pay
phone.

"He just dropped a dime in the water fountain," one of
them says. "He's going tonight."

"And I know who's going with him," the other coach says.

14

They hear the shower clogs coming back and they watch him pass the door. They go to bed and one of them gets up at 2 A.M. and checks the room, and our parched hero, who stood there like that small boy and asked for that drink of water, and his roommate are both gone.

"I've got to go tonight," another finally announces to his associates every year. "I've just got to try him."

So he tries me, some of his clothes and some towels rolled up to bulk like his body under the covers of his bed, and I knick him. It's a game, and in my struggle to understand it I am reminded of something Lou Little once said about his Columbia football players to Frank Graham, the New York sports columnist.

"When I see them on the field they look like gladiators," Lou said, "but when I see them off the field they're just kids."

9:02 A.M.

I stop at the counter in the main office to pick up the *Milwaukee Sentinel*, the *Chicago Tribune* and the *Chicago Sun-Times*. On the counter there is a pound can of pipe tobacco and, wrapped in waxed paper, a dill pickle. Tom Fears coaches our receivers and he smokes a pipe and has a dill pickle for lunch every day. For nine seasons with the Los Angeles Rams he was one of the league's great receivers, and he caught an even 400 passes. In 1950 he caught eighteen in one game against the Packers for a league record. He has six children and his wife will be moving five of them East with her at the end of the month. The other is Pat, who came into training camp with his father on July 15. He is eight years old and, on the players' weight chart in the dressing room, he is listed at 69 pounds, but he has the appetite of a tackle.

"Have we had lunch yet?" he said to someone on the practice field one day.

"No," the other said. "We just had breakfast."

"Oh," Pat said. "I was wondering if dinner is next."

9:15 A.M.

I have looked through the sports pages and I see that Paul Dudley, who was a fourth draft pick for us and one of our first-year men this year, scored his first touchdown for the

15

Giants. He couldn't break into our backfield but he's got good speed and fine moves and he's rugged enough and he's a good one, and every time you trade off one of those, because you happen to be deep at the moment, you wonder if you're not making a mistake, if he might be even better than you think and you'll be haunted by him for years. This year they're haunting Paul Brown for having traded Bobby Mitchell, but it could happen to me.

In the stories about our game with the Bears the papers all say the same thing, each in their own words. We're "power-packed" and "precision-timed" or "all-powerful" or "indestructible." They don't overlook that the Bears were hurt coming in, but that 49-0 score in the big black numbers in the headlines makes us look better than we are and I wish we had a couple of those touchdowns in the bank for this week.

9:20 A.M.

Bud Lea of the *Milwaukee Sentinel* and Gene Hintz of United Press International come in, and I have been told that any time a sportswriter asks me a question I almost visibly flinch. I haven't been hurt yet and I've had the best press anyone can expect, but the off-the-cuff statement is not one of my big plays. I have seen too many seemingly sound statements blow up in the faces of too many sound coaches and I'm not at my best when I'm walking off the practice field, honestly feeling that my whole future will depend upon my discovery of some way to rearrange our blocking on our 49-Sweep to take care of some particular beast of a linebacker, and a sportswriter comes up to me and says, "Well, coach, what do you think today?"

The problem with the press this week, after that 49 to 0, will be to convince them I mean it when I say that if we don't play our best game of the season on Sunday, these other people will knock us on our tails. Bud Lea and Gene Hintz start out asking me about injuries.

"Tom Moore has a muscle pull in his shoulder," I say, "and Hornung pulled a groin muscle. I think they'll be in shape, but I don't know."

It's an odd thing about that Moore. He was the first ballplayer I ever drafted for the Packers. He was our number one draft choice in 1960 and I've never regretted it. He's got

16

good size and speed and power, and in his first year scored five touchdowns and caught five passes and led the league in kickoff returns. I have had to play him behind Jim Taylor at fullback, or Hornung at halfback, and the odd thing is that, when one or the other is hurt and I send in Moore, he gets banged up, too. He is an upright runner, and I wouldn't change that for a minute because it's his way of going, but I've got to get him to button up as he gets hit, which is something that Taylor does instinctively and Hornung has mastered. You can't go in there upright in this league without getting racked.

"If I know Paul Hornung," Bud Lea says, "he'll be ready, if it's possible."

If I, too, know Paul Hornung he'll be ready because this is one of those great money ballplayers, but he was in the army for nine months, seven of them after the season ended. From June into the third week in July the newspapers were carrying rumors of when he would get out and, finally, one evening of our second week in camp he showed up and I saw him getting out of his car in front of Sensenbrenner Hall.

It was dark by then and he walked over into the light from the doorway. You have to know what Paul Hornung means to this team to read all the meaning into the searching inspection I was giving him. I have heard and read that Paul Hornung is not a great runner or a great passer or a great field-goal kicker, although no one can fault him as a great blocker, but he led the league in scoring for three seasons; in 1960 he broke Don Hutson's all-time league seasonal scoring record with 176 points and he was twice voted the league's outstanding player. What it comes down to is that in the middle of the field he may be only slightly better than an average ballplayer, but inside that 20-yard line he is one of the greatest I've ever seen. He smells that goal line. Henry Jordan, our defensive right tackle, expressed what Hornung means to our team when he said, "Before our 1961 championship game I was under the impression that Moore could run as well as Hornung and that Ben Agajanian could kick as well or better, but the week before the game, when Paul got that leave from the army and walked into that locker room, you could just feel the confidence grow in that room."

We were shaking hands now in the light from that doorway, and he had on dark gray slacks and a T-shirt. He is not a Spartan liver and there were those months in the army and I was looking for fat.

"What do you weigh?" I said.

"Oh, about 222," he said. "I'm only about seven pounds over."

"Good," I said, and that's what I thought. He checked in then and for four or five days on that practice field I watched him building himself back in shape. Late in practice on the fifth or sixth day just before sending them in, we lined up our kickoff team against our receiving team. They were all in shorts and T-shirts, just to run through it and to reacquaint them with their assignments after seven months, and Paul, in a sweatsuit, was the deep man to the right in the end zone.

"Watch this," someone on the sideline said. "Aggie will kick it to Hornung to make him run."

Agajanian was in camp to work with our kickers, and he booted it to Paul, who took it about 5 yards deep in the end zone. He tucked it in and started out and was great for the first 15 yards. At the 20-yard line he was absolutely coming apart. He was trying to get his knees up and the effort was almost bending him over backward and he looked like he was a participant in a potato race at an Elks picnic.

"All the way!" I was shouting at him. "Run it all the way to that goal line!"

On the sideline now some of the other players were cat-calling and whistling at Paul Hornung. Watching him, barely able to run, all I could think was: Can this be the famous "Golden Boy"? Can this be the most valuable player in the National Football League, the most publicized ballplayer in pro football, that runner, blocker, kicker and great competitor on whom so much depends if we are going to hold on to that title? And I closed practice.

"Well," I said to him, walking off the field, "I guess you got the news."

"I got it," he said, trying to get his breath, the sweat running off his face.

"That was ludicrous," I said. "That was absurd. What the blast have you been doing with yourself?"

"I don't know," he said. "I don't know."

This is a man with great pride, I knew, and he loves this game, and that would have to be the saver. When the Packers drafted him in 1957 he was All-America at Notre Dame for two years and the Heisman Trophy winner his last year and he came here preceded by all that publicity. They tried him at quarterback and then fullback, and like many a great college star who does not make it big with the pros he fell

18

into that what's-it-to-you attitude that they erect as a defensive perimeter around their egos.

When I joined this club in 1959 Paul Hornung was more celebrated for his reputed exploits off the field than on, but after the months I had spent studying the movies of Packer games I knew that one of the ballplayers I needed was Paul Hornung. With those I could take into my confidence I investigated meticulously that reputation and I found that, although Paul Hornung had given the gossips cause, their malicious imaginations had taken it the rest of the way, and the first talk I ever had with him was right here in this office and it was about that reputation.

"If that's the way they want to think," he said, "that's the way they'll think."

I liked the way he looked me right smack in the eye and I found that, while you have to whip him a little, he is no malingerer. This is a good-looking, intelligent and charming celebrity whom I can't expect to lead the life of a monk, but he is also a dedicated ballplayer who, pre-season, will run up and down those steep steps of City Stadium to get his legs in shape—and we'll need him this Sunday.

9:35 A.M.

After the press leaves, Tom Miller brings in the play-by-play of the Bears game. During the mid-Forties he played end for the Eagles, the Redskins and the Packers and he is our publicity man. Each Monday he goes over the play-by-play, marking the most significant plays on the left border of his copy, and then I go over it and mark what I think were the key plays on the right border for my weekly television show.

"There's no shortage this week," he says. "With the seven touchdowns and three interceptions, that fumble recovery and a lot of other things they're going to have to do some cutting."

My show will never challenge "Meet The Press" as a public affairs program, but they seem to like it around here. Al Sampson, one of the local sports commentators, shoots the film and each Wednesday evening Don Hutson, the great former end of the Packers, one of my coaches and I go into that studio at WBAY-TV and try not to look and sound like the Three Stooges.

9:55 A.M.

I tell Ruth McCloskey, my secretary, that I'm leaving for the stadium, but she is still being pestered for tickets for Sunday's game and we try to solve that. When I walk into the main office, Verne Lewellen comes out of his office. From 1924 through 1932, in those days of low-score football, he racked up fifty touchdowns for Green Bay and it is still a record for a Packer back. He is now our business manager.

"We're all out of our allotted tickets for the Eagles game," he says, "and I'm still getting player requests."

"Look," I say. "That's five weeks away and we're playing it in Philadelphia, which is a thousand miles away."

"I know," he says, "but there are a lot of them with a lot of friends in the East."

"You handle it any way you can," I say. "I've got my own problems."

10:12 A.M.

I drive one block out South Washington Street and turn right over the Mason Street Bridge. The weather is still good, but there is a slight haze over everything now. Yesterday it was so clear that the sky was like a blue bowl over the stadium. It will not surprise me if we get rain for this next one, and I doubt that anyone in this league ever wants rain. We all draw our plays on dry paper and we count on the ability of our backs and our receivers to make their cuts on a dry field. I don't think that there is a mud-thinker among us, because we all have to conceive of this game as it should be played.

As I turn onto Oneida Avenue, the two practice fields, the camera tower between them, are on the left, the low green bleachers, empty now, along the avenue, and the stadium are on the right atop the rise of the vacant parking fields. For every hour of game play that we put in at that stadium and at the others around the league, we put in fourteen on those fields. That is pre-season and during the season, and then there are those equal hours spent in those meetings, and all of this does not include the time we coaches spend in preparation for those practice sessions and those meetings, and that time seems to me to be almost incalculable.

I see my coaches' cars and maybe a half dozen others parked outside now, and I walk through the empty dressing room and into the trainer's room. Tom Moore is sitting on one of the rubbing tables, stripped to the waist, and Bud Jorgensen, our trainer, is using the diathermy on Moore's shoulder.

"How does it feel?" I say.

"Not so good," Moore says. "It's pretty sore right now."

"Will he be all right?" I say to Jorgensen.

"I think so," he says.

"How about Hornung?" I say. "Is he in yet?"

"No," Jorgensen says. "He'll be in later. The pull isn't in the groin, it's inside the thigh."

Every week there are the injuries. It is foolish to think that, the way this game is played, you can escape them, but every week I feel that same annoyance, and I need Hornung and I need Moore if we are going to beat these people.

"Gentlemen," I say, when I walk into the coaches' room, "that was a good game yesterday."

They are all there—Bill Austin and Norb Hecker and Phil Bengston and Tom Fears and Red Cochran. Phil coaches the defensive line and linebackers, Norb the defensive backs, Bill the offensive line, Red the offensive backfield and Tom handles those receivers.

"It wasn't a bad one, at that," Phil says. He was an All-America tackle at Minnesota in 1933–34, and coached college ball under Don Faurot at Missouri and Clark Shaughnessy at Stanford. For eight years, before I got him, he coached the line for the Forty-Niners, and he is not given to exaggeration. "I thought we looked pretty good out there."

"You really think that was pretty good?" Red Cochran says. "Pretty good?"

He is out of the Carolinas and was a back at Wake Forest and, from 1947 through 1950, with the Chicago Cardinals. He coached the backfield for five years at Wake Forest and for three with the Lions. Putting this staff together in 1959, I met him for the first time between planes in that remodeled hangar at the old Willow Run airport in Detroit. We were to have an hour between planes, but ours was fifty minutes late and, as we were coming in, I asked Marie to take care of the tickets for the flight out for Green Bay so that I could have at least five minutes with Red Cochran.

21

"I don't know this Red Cochran," she said, "but I know you. All I can hope for him is that he's not sitting in the bar but that he's waiting at the gate."

He was waiting at the gate.

"Well," I say to Bill Austin, "let's look at them, and I hope we're not disappointed."

Once a game is won and in the bank I would rather not look at the movies. No matter how good we look on the field I can find so many things wrong in the pictures.

"If we're not disappointed," Bill Austin says, "it'll be the first time."

Bill Austin played four years at tackle for Oregon State and in 1949, although he was only 20, he was first-string with the Giants. He put in three years in service and was All-Pro offensive guard with the Giants when I coached their offense. I got him from Wichita, where he was coaching the line, and he is our resident authority on the significance of approaching weather fronts and our first-string motion-picture projectionist.

"Look at this!" I'm saying now, watching Ronnie Bull of the Bears take Willie Wood's kickoff and bring it back to the Bears' 37. "We are absolutely the world's worst team on covering kicks. What have we got those two men sitting on the outside for?"

The kickoff is always a scary play, but there is equal nervousness on both sides. You try to get all the speed you can into your kickoff team, because it's a sprint for everyone, but you cannot sacrifice size. You need that size, particularly in the middle to meet their wedge, and you put your two real speed burners as the third men in from either sideline. They are the ones who have to force the action, who must make the other people show their play, and your two outside men have to be strong enough and active enough to keep that play to the inside. Those outside men have got to stay upright and protect those sidelines, but they can't be so sideline-conscious that they just stand around out there like a couple of program venders.

I throw the switch and reverse the projector. They are all running backward now and the ball is leaving Bull's hands and returning to Willie Wood's toe, and I run it again.

"Look at this," I say again, a half dozen plays later. "You can see Hornung pull up with that muscle."

Bart Starr fakes a handoff to Hornung, and Paul actually executes his own fake into the line with so much sincerity

22

that you can see he has pulled that muscle and is in pain. The play is a swing pass to Jimmy Taylor to the left but the pass doesn't lead Jimmy enough and he tries to turn for it and drops the ball.

That's a problem with Taylor, and sincerity costs us twice on that one play. He's not big for a fullback—6 feet and 212 pounds—but he is so sincere in that all-year muscle-building program of his that when you bump against him it's like bumping into a cast-iron statue. Nothing gives, and he has developed those neck muscles to the point where, when he wants to turn his head, he has to turn his whole upper body.

"What's the matter with you?" I said to him on the practice field the other day when he couldn't turn for the ball on that very play. "Can't you twist your head?"

"You just can't make a greyhound out of a bulldog, coach," he said.

And he is a bulldog. Your fullback must be big enough to make the tough yardage, have enough speed to go the distance when you break him into the clear and he should, as should all backs, have that real quick start. He should be a great blocker, because he is that remaining back on passes, when the center and the fullback pick up the red-doggers. He must have good enough hands to go out on pass routes, too, because if he hasn't it won't be long before the other defenses learn to ignore him as they do some fullbacks.

In an open field our James is something else again. I think that when he sees a clear field ahead he hunts down somebody to run into, and while you have to enjoy body contact to play this game, Jimmy exults in it. After one of our 1960 games with the Bears I made him watch himself on the film going out of the way to run over Charlie Sumner, who was then their weak-side safety.

"What were you trying to do out there?" I said.

"You gotta sting 'em a little, coach," Jimmy said. "You know you've gotta make those tacklers respect you."

They respect him. In fact, every time he carries the ball there are eleven of them, all of whom want to pay their respects to him personally, and in our game with the Rams in 1961 in Los Angeles I remember four of them nailing him right in front of the Rams' bench.

"How to go, you guys!" they tell me Jimmy said when he jumped up. "That's the way to play this game!"

Now, if I could just get him to block with the same abandon, he might be the best in the business. He is not a bad

23

blocker, but he would be a great one with his ruggedness, his quickness and his agility, if they would just change the rules to let him carry a football while he's blocking.

On the screen now Bart Starr is faking to Tom Moore, who went in for Hornung, and then he drops back and throws toward Max McGee, our split left end, who had run a Zig-In pass route. Max has a step on Dave Whitsell, but Starr's pass is behind him and Whitsell intercepts.

Bart's too tense, I'm thinking. I noticed it last week and the week before, and I can understand it because there is no one on this team who is more conscientious and dedicated than Bart Starr. By the nature of his position your quarterback is your number one man, and we are the champions and I know that Bart feels that he has the whole burden of our offense on his shoulders and I will have to try to relax him.

When I joined this team the opinion around here and in the league was that Starr would never make it. They said he couldn't throw well enough and wasn't tough enough, that he had no confidence in himself and that no one had confidence in him. He was a top student at Alabama so they said he was smart enough, and after looking at the movies that first pre-season I came to the conclusion that he did have the ability—the arm, the ball-handling techniques and the intelligence—but what he needed was confidence.

He is the son of a regular army master sergeant and he grew up on army posts and air force bases and he still calls me "sir." When I first met him he struck me as so polite and so self-effacing that I wondered if maybe he wasn't too nice a boy to be the authoritarian leader that your quarterback must be.

He impressed me getting ready for our first pre-season game in 1959. At our quarterback meetings, even though he was not first-string, he could repeat almost verbatim everything we had discussed the previous three days, and that meant he had a great memory, dedication and desire. He is also a great student of the game, always borrowing movies from our film library during the season and between seasons, to take them home and study them over and over, and with our success and his own success I have seen his confidence grow.

"A couple of years ago," he said to me the day last summer when he brought his contract into the office, "I'd have signed anything you gave me, but now you've taught me

Willie Davis is working for his master's degree i̶n̶ [obscured]tion, and his gratitude to pro ball is expressed in his wh̶o̶le [obscured] attitude toward the game. He has never smoked and, as he says, "I'm not considered a drinker." Between games, and even in the off-season, he replays game situations over and over in his mind, analyzing his errors.

"I try to play," he says, "so I can live with myself."

Of course, he's a worrier, not worried about the team winning, but about how Willie Davis will play. Like most ballplayers he doesn't eat much before a game, but often he can't eat after a game until the next day, and Willie Davis is another one I'll have to try to keep loose going into this game.

"See this?" I'm saying now, watching that screen as the Bears kick and Willie Wood takes it on our 23 and starts upfield. "If Gremminger throws his block, Willie would know which way to go."

Willie Wood and Hank Gremminger are in our defensive backfield with Jesse Whittenton and Herb Adderley, and John Symank in reserve. Willie, at 5-10, is the shortest man on our squad, and he weighs only 185. When he was a quarterback and defensive back at Southern California, our scouts said he was too small and that he didn't have enough speed. No one drafted Willie but he wrote letters to all the clubs and, because we were so desperate for defensive backs in 1960, we invited him to camp. They were right about his size and his lack of top speed, but what they didn't know is that he can jump like a gazelle. He can touch the crossbar on the goalposts with his wrist and he has great timing and that sixth sense for being in the right place at the right time. He is the most natural defensive back we have, and Mike Ditka of the Bears has said that no one has ever tackled him harder than our little Willie.

The first time we ever used Willie Wood, though, was against the Colts in Baltimore, and Willie said later he thought that was the end for him. In this league when you put in a first-year man, especially at defensive back and particularly a corner man, they love to go to work on him. They hit for four touchdowns right over Willie, but the one I remember was a draw fake and Willie came up and tackled the fullback and Johnny Unitas hit Ray Berry 30 yards behind Willie, and that just about took us out of it.

They have to learn by experience, though, and Willie is a smart one. After the season he teaches science and math in junior high school in Washington, and the day we lucked into

enough to make you wonder. It costs us well over
$50,000 a year to scout the colleges and we got Willie
through a letter he wrote and mailed with a 4-cent stamp.

If Willie Wood is a natural, I would say that no one has
worked harder at making himself a fine defensive back than
Hank Gremminger. Hank just won't take your word for anything. You have to prove it to him and, unlike some of them,
he's mature enough to take criticism. He was an offensive end
at Baylor, so he's got the agility and the hands and the timing you need, and he's a great student of his opponent. The
odd thing about him is that he's high-strung and nervous and
tends to brood when he gets beat by a receiver. That's unusual among defensive backs, because when you get beat back
there you have to forget it and concentrate on the next play.

That kick to Willie Wood is the last play of the first quarter. In the second quarter we score both times we get the
ball, and the key play is our L and R, or crossing ends, play,
the 46-yard touchdown pass from Starr to Ron Kramer, our
big tight end, that takes us into the dressing room ahead
14-0. It looked great from the sideline, but now on the
screen I see that Max McGee, our split end to the left,
didn't take their right corner man deep enough with him. He
made his move to the inside too soon, and the only reason
Ron was able to go all the way was that he is big enough
and strong enough to run right through that man.

"Do you want lunch now?" Norb Hecker says, while Bill
Austin is rewinding the reel. "I think it's out there."

Norb Hecker made Little All-America at Baldwin Wallace
and for six years was a fine defensive back with the Rams
and the Redskins. He was a player-coach in the Canadian
league in 1959 when I grabbed him. He not only has the
brains and the enthusiasm, but also the patience to drill
those defensive backs over and over on those key and zone
and man-to-man and combination defenses that we use, and
on the pass-pattern preferences of the other people and the
manner in which the individual receivers like to run their
routes.

So we eat our hamburgers and Tom Fears has his dill
pickle and then we watch the second half. I see us score five
more touchdowns, but I see Bart Starr is ignoring our quick
man, the tight end, on our Flood pass and that the quick man
will always be open before the deep man is. I see that our
guards aren't always pulling out of there as they should and
that on our sweep right our blocking back has got to stop

28

cutting off our lead guard. I mean he has to get to his man quicker. That's why, even when we win by seven touchdowns, my instincts are to resist looking at those movies. When you walk off the field after a game like that you think they looked great and you can only be disappointed. The satisfactions are few, I guess, for perfectionists, but I have never known a good coach who wasn't one.

"All right," I say. "It's almost one o'clock, so let's get on with the real business."

It is the same every week. You spend six days building for one opponent, and on Monday you have to forget it. Win or lose, if you don't put it behind you, you'll be wading around all week, knee deep in confusion. So now we will look at the other people who are coming in here Sunday, and Bill Austin puts on the first reel of their game of eight days ago against the San Francisco Forty-Niners.

It is just Bill Austin, Red Cochran, Tom Fears and me now, and the film has been edited so that we see our opponent only on defense. In the visitors' dressing room Phil Bengston and Norb Hecker have the other portions, so that while we are putting in our offense they can be working out our defenses against our opponent's offensive plays.

"Right end, 89," Bill Austin says. "Right tackle, 76."

"Left end, 78," Tom Fears says. "Left tackle, 71. Middle linebacker, 56."

While they watch the first Forty-Niner play, Austin and Fears call off the jersey numbers and positions of the other people and Red Cochran lists them on the first of the many sheets of lined, yellow, legal-pad paper we will fill this week.

"Forty-Niners in Red Right," Austin says.

I do not believe this game is as complex as many people think it is and as some try to make it. At the same time I don't think it is as simple as it was twenty years ago. We try to make it as uncomplicated as we can, because I believe that if you block and tackle better than the other team and the breaks are even you're going to win, but we can't make it quite as simple as playground tag, and what Bill Austin has called off is the first Forty-Niner formation.

We have four basic offensive formations and they are standard in this league. In Red Right the fullback takes his position not in a line with the quarterback and the center, as he does in Black, Brown and Blue formations, but almost directly behind our right tackle. Any play may be run from any one of these formations, the halfback positions varying in the others. Bill Austin has called off the formation because it is not the play but rather the formation that dictates the defense.

"4–3," Tom Fears says, calling off the defensive alignment.

We record the position of the ball on the field, the down and yardage, as well as the formation and the defense, on each play. In this way we build up our whole picture of their defensive preferences, what defenses they use under what situations, so that on Wednesday we will be able to sit down with our offensive team and say that, in a certain situation, the other people can be expected to be in a certain defense 85 or 90 or 95 percent of the time.

"That 56 is just as fast as ever," I say, "and they get a lot of pursuit out of that 71."

They are the two best the defense has up front, and that 56 is disarming. He is rather round-faced and soft looking and he does not impress you off the field, but on it he is as good a middle linebacker as there is in the business. That 71 is just a great tackle, and those are the two who will plague me most of all.

"The right end should be open for something," Tom Fears says, meaning the Forty-Niner right end, but thinking of our Ron Kramer. "The middle and right linebackers pull off to the left."

"But there's no use flying him," I say, meaning there is no point in just sending him straight downfield at full speed and without a fake. "That left safety will just pick him up."

We have twenty-five pass routes for our ends and our wingback, or flanker. We have fifteen for our remaining backs, our halfback and our fullback. Then there are our combination patterns, but there are some that you know right away are dead against certain secondaries and others that you can forget on a certain Sunday because of specific characteristics of the individuals in that secondary. There are some defensive halfbacks or safety men whom you may beat short but never long, or long but never short, or outside but never inside or inside short but never outside short. And that is another reason why I say this has become a game for madmen.

"I don't know whether that 81 thinks he's slowing up," I say, meaning their left defensive halfback, "but he's giving a lot more room than he used to."

"He's 10 yards off that flanker," Red Cochran says.

"He may be slowing up," Bill Austin says, "but not much."

"He's still quick as a cat," I say. "Let's think."

Bill Austin stops the projector and Tom Fears turns on the ceiling light. We have a multiple number of plays, but you don't begin to give them all to the team. Regardless of what you do put in, every game boils down to doing the things you do best and doing them over and over again. We have seven plays to get us around end and there are two or three ways of blocking each. One of the plays is our 29, our pitch-out to Jimmy Taylor, and I want us to stop right here and think a little about any adjustments we might make in blocking against the defenses we have seen the defense deploy up to now on the screen.

"Maybe if we release that end," I say, meaning our tight end, Ron Kramer, "that safety man won't come up as fast."

"Let Dowler crack back on that left linebacker," Bill Austin says.

I diagram it and we talk it over. I would like to free Ron Kramer from that blocking assignment and release him downfield to give the pitchout the appearance of a pass, and after we rearrange the blocking Bill Austin starts the projector again.

"We shouldn't have any trouble with our pass blocking," I say. "They're not doing anything of consequence that I can see."

The most difficult thing we have to teach our offensive linemen is pass protection. When they come to us their experience is limited by the fact that 75 percent of the passes thrown in college evolve out of their running game and they use aggressive-type blocks up front. We use drop-back protection, either man-to-man or area, to form that pocket, and it is not easy to teach that upright, ground-giving but still tenacious block that we demand. To these aggressive types who play this game the concept of retreat is odd and unnatural, but we want aggressive retreat, and it is all the same thing: "This is a personal battle between him and your opponent."

"All right," I say. "It's four-fifteen. Let's knock off now."

We have run that film through, backing it up and starting some plays over sometimes three or four times. We have taken off the defenses the opponent used against the formations and in what situations, and we have started to list our plays that appear plausible against them. I know right now that, by tomorrow night, we are going to have too many again and we'll have to start discarding. When

31

I walk into the visitors' dressing room Phil Bengtson and Norb Hecker have finished taking off the offensive formations and plays the other people used against the Forty-Niners and Phil is plotting them.

"Do we get this week's game tonight?" he says.

"It's due in at the airport at seven-thirty," Red Cochran says.

For each game we exchange the films of our last two games. At the end of last week a print of our game with the Cardinals two weeks ago went from the Bears to these other people, who are studying it right now, and today a print of our Bears game of yesterday was shipped out to them by priority air express. We got this film of their Forty-Niner game from the Colts, who played these people last week, and after we are finished with the film of that game with the Colts we will send it on Friday to the Rams, who will be in Washington, because they play them the week after we do. There are films flying back and forth across this country all fall, and it is a complicated procedure that Red Cochran has to work out when the league schedule is announced each spring.

6 P.M.

Tim Cohane is in town and, because I have less than an hour for dinner, we decide to eat at his motel. In my senior year at Fordham he was the college public relations man and, although he didn't dream up "The Seven Blocks of Granite" he did more than anyone else to popularize that title they hung on us linemen. He is sports editor of *Look* and the best friend I have among the press, and we get into a hassle over the proofs of an article on which he and Paul Hornung have collaborated.

"I don't like some of this," I say.

It is typical of Hornung's frankness. He looks the reader right in the eye. It is undoubtedly an honest and excellent piece and Hornung has every right to reveal what he wants to about himself but, it seems to me, I have to protest when, by name or inference, he involves others who have no opportunity to retort.

"You're getting just like all the rest of them," Tim says, exploding.

"Will you let me say something?" I say.

"All you people—you coaches and you athletes—are all alike," Tim says. "Everything is fine as long as we write a lot of pandering pap extolling you as heroes and publicizing your game, but the moment we write something that doesn't make you look like tin gods you get your backs up."

"Will you listen to me?" I say.

"Well, I want to tell you I've had it," Tim says. "If you're getting as narrow-minded as the rest of them and can't see the virtues of this piece it's the end of the road for me."

. We work it out. We have too much respect for each other not to, so I give a little and Tim recognizes a point or two of mine, and we agree that it is still a forthright and fascinating article.

6:55 P.M.

I walk around the corner to the office and up the stairs to the coaches' rooms. Phil Bengston, Bill Austin, Norb Hecker and Tom Fears are there, and Wally Cruice is sitting on Phil's desk talking with them.

Wally Cruice is our scout, and yesterday he was in Baltimore watching the other team against the Colts. He was a back at Northwestern and has been scouting for the Packers since 1947, and he is the best I have ever known. It is a complex job because on every play he must check the down and distance and position on the field, break down the offense and defense into formations and, at the same time, be looking for individual characteristics or tip-offs. Only experience tells him where to look and what to ignore, and he has only twenty-five seconds while the ball is dead between plays to get it all down on paper. If he sees a play he does not recognize immediately he must, in just the few seconds it takes it to unfold, spot the key to it so that he can diagram, for example, who is pulling and who isn't. After the game he flies home to put in seven or eight hours making out the report he submits to us on Monday night and delivers to the team on Tuesday.

"What about their quarterback?" I ask Wally. They traded their quarterback during the off-season and their new one came out of the Eastern Division of the league. Naturally, we have not had the opportunity to see as much of him as we have of the other quarterbacks we play against.

"He's primarily interested in percentage," Wally says,

33

meaning percentage of pass completions. "That's his bible. He'll go for the long one against you once in a while, but it's basically percentage and possession."

"Have you got anything here on what the Colts did against them?"

"You asked for it," Wally says, "so I brought it along."

The game this Sunday has been bothering me since the end of last season. I felt then and I know now that if we are going to win the title again, we must beat this team, and so I gave Wally an extra burden. Normally he concentrates only on the people we are playing the next week, but this time I asked him to chart the Colts' offense against them as well to save us the time it would take us to get it off the film.

He hands me a half dozen sheets covering eighteen Baltimore plays. He has them diagrammed and I glance at them and put them aside for tomorrow.

"What are we looking at now?" I say to Bill Austin. Phil Bengtson and Norb Hecker have one projector set up in the coaches' office and Bill and Tom Fears and Wally and I are in the back room.

"Their pre-season game this year with Cleveland," Bill says.

We watch that, running it back and forth for an hour, taking off their defenses against formations again. At eight-fifteen Red Cochran comes in from the airport where he went to get the film of their game of yesterday in Baltimore.

"You get it?" I say.

"No," Red says. "It wasn't on the plane."

"Any more flights from there tonight?"

"No," Red says, and I know we've had it again. "There's a flight coming in from Chicago that gets in after nine, but it won't be on that. It'll probably be in at eight-thirty to-morrow morning."

"All right," I say, "let's get our pass protection down so we know what we're going to do."

Red and Bill go to the blackboard and diagram six pass-blocking methods. We work out our protection against their various defenses and dependent upon what man or com-bination of men they blitz.

"We're stymied for tonight," I say when we finish that, "unless we look at one of our own films against them."

"Which one do you want?" Bill Austin says. "I suppose the first?"

"Yes," I say.

"It'll make you sick," Bill says.

"I can stand to get sick," I say.

So I have to see it again, that first game last year, when they beat us 17-13. I have to see them score after those two broken plays and I have to see us get stopped again twice inside their 5-yard line.

"Put down that 67 from the Red," I say to Bill Austin, watching again one of our plays from inside the 5 that should have gone.

"Everybody in the line gets a 2," Red Cochran says. It is the way we grade our offensive blocking, with a 1 meaning 50 percent and 2 standing for perfect. "Even then we don't score."

"Jimmy Taylor runs the wrong hole," I say. We number our holes 8-6-4-2-0 from the left and 1-3-5-7-9 to the right. On that 67 Jimmy should have taken the 7 hole, off the right shoulder of our closed right end, but he thought he saw daylight at the 5 hole over right tackle and when he got there he found out he was wrong.

"All right," I say finally, looking at my watch. "It's five after eleven so that's enough for tonight."

Driving home ten minutes later, the only lights I see are those of the Fort Howard Paper Company across the Fox River, but I derive small comfort from the realization that we're not the only ones working on this night.

TUESDAY

7:40 A.M.

Marie is coming down with a heavy cold or the flu, but I have done so much talking about the necessity of ignoring the small hurts that it has even pervaded our household and she refuses to go to the doctor. Her excuse is that this afternoon she is having that tea at the Oneida Country Club for the team wives, and I remember having seen around the house somewhere in the last day or so a table centerpiece she has been working on, the broad leaves of it lettered with the names of our opponents.

A professional football team is a kind of community of displaced persons. A few of them and their families live in the Green Bay area the year around, but the rest are here only from July through December. When the first-year men are single or newly married it is comparatively simple to find them apartments, but as their families grow through the years it is a problem to find them suitable houses and there is a mad scramble every summer. They come from all over the country and some of the wives have never before left the towns where they were born. Often they are homesick and unhappy with local customs or local climate. But I think it eased the problem a little last year when, after we won the championship, we gave each of them a mink stole, and that Oneida Country Club will probably look like a mink ranch this afternoon.

"So at least I can drop Susan off at school," I say to Marie.

7:50 A.M.

Inside their own 10, I am thinking now, driving with Susan, they are the toughest team in football to move. That left tackle, that 71, is as good a defensive tackle as there is and he will give anybody trouble and Jerry Kramer has to handle him.

"Daddy!" Susan says. "You're forgetting me again."

I have started to pass Susan's school corner, so I let her out at the opposite curb. At the traffic light I am held up by a trailer loaded with Holsteins trying to make the turn—and Jerry will handle that 71 as well as anybody because nothing intimidates Jerry, and if you told him he had to throw a block on that trailer he'd give it a try.

Jerry Kramer has the perfect devil-may-care attitude it takes to play this game. He not only ignores the small hurts but the large ones, too, and the evidence of his indifference is all over his body.

When Jerry was a high school kid he was sanding a lamp in the woodworking shop one Friday afternoon and a lathe took a couple of inches of flesh out of his side and he played football that night. On a duck-hunting trip he shredded his right forearm with a shot gun blast, and once, when a rotten board split under him, a sliver went into his groin. He pulled that out and two days later they found seven and a half inches of it still in there. He was in the hospital for two weeks, but three weeks later he was playing football. Then there was the night he was in a car doing 100 miles an hour and it went off the road. He was thrown out of the car. It rolled over him, hit a tree and burst into flames. He walked away from it.

At three o'clock one morning at the University of Idaho, Jerry bet somebody he could ring the bell on the roof of one of the dorms. He threw a rope on the railing around the cupola and while he was dangling three stories above the ground the railing started to give. If a couple of them looking out of a window hadn't grabbed the rope he would probably have walked away from that, too. In 1960 he suffered a concussion and a detached retina in his left eye in one of our games and had to undergo a four-and-a-half-hour operation. And in 1961 against the Minnesota Vikings he broke his left ankle and had to wear a 2-inch pin in there for four months.

"But where'd you get that big scar on the back of your neck?" someone asked him once. Because of it they call him Zipper Head.

"Where the hell *did* I get that?" Jerry said, and he wasn't kidding. This typifies him. "Oh yeah, I remember now. In my sophomore year in college I couldn't turn my head and they X-rayed it and found out I had a chipped vertebra."

I remember our Dallas game a couple of years ago and on our 49-Sweep Jerry got two defenders and picked up a piece of a third. We were playing the Forty-Niners later and they say Red Hickey, their coach, was screening our game and he called his staff in and said, "My God! Just look at this guard!"

8:27 A.M.

After eight o'clock Mass at St. Willebrord's I drive across the Mason Street Bridge, and for the first time I am aware that the bad weather that started yesterday has continued and that it is a gray day. I stop for breakfast at Sneezer's—a name that charms Tim Cohane—on Route 41 and get the *Milwaukee Sentinel* at the stand outside and sit down at the counter.

"The same?" the waitress says.

"Yes, please," I say. I have opened to the sports page and I see the headline over Bud Lea's story:

Is this what I want? I want them to believe in themselves, to believe that they can beat anyone, but just because we beat the crippled Bears 49 to 0 I don't want us strutting and spreading overconfidence.

"We're just too strong up front," Jimmy Taylor is saying in the first paragraph. "We've got the horses in the backfield. When we make up our mind to move, there's not a defense in the league that will stop us."

This defense we're meeting on Sunday may stop us. If we sashay in there thinking it's going to be last Sunday all over again, they'll stop us, but it's a funny thing about Jimmy Taylor. When our new regime came in here in 1959 he'd give you a limp handshake and hardly say anything. Now when you shake hands with him he almost drives you to your knees, and his confidence even shows in the paper.

That's what success did for him, and Jerry Kramer helped, too. When you see Jimmy Taylor run right into and over somebody on the field you wouldn't think that he'd always be seeking friendship and understanding. He has a great need for both, however, and he and Jerry hit it off and room together in training camp. Jerry brings his hi-fi into camp and an armful of good books. Last summer he was reading Steinbeck and O'Hara and he had Jimmy reading *The Family Book of Best Loved Poems*.

We used to have to scurry to find personal incentives for Jimmy, too, to get him up psychologically Sunday after Sunday. Now the race for league ground-gaining honors he's been having with Jimmy Brown supplies that and he'll be up for this one.

"Morning, coach."

"Hello, Fuzz," I say.

Fuzzy Thurston has come in and is sitting at the other counter. When I see him I am reminded of that right tackle, that 76, he'll have to block on Sunday. That 76 stands 6-5 and weighs 300 pounds. When he first came up two years ago I didn't believe the program listing, but then he walked by me on the field, towering over me, and with the calves of his legs as big as my thighs. And he can move, too.

Fuzzy never played any high school football or college football until his coach at Valparaiso picked him off a basketball floor in Fuzzy's junior year. He had been kicked around a lot before we got him from the Colts.

"I'll tell you what it comes down to," Fuzzy says. "When you've been cut four times and have a wife and two kids you've just got to make it. You don't only owe it to your family, you owe it to your life."

He has made it big with us. When we traded for him we'd seen just enough in movies to know he could handle the pass block, but we didn't know if he had the speed to pull and we knew nothing about his personality. He's not quite as good a pulling guard as Jerry Kramer, but he's a good short-trap blocker and he's got enough quickness, size, strength and determination so that, when he and Jerry come swinging around that corner together like a pair of matched Percherons, you can see that defensive man's eyeballs pop.

Fuzzy's pass-protection blocking, though, is his big card, and he is as good as anyone in the league. Nobody gives him trouble on that, and if he's right on Sunday he'll handle that big 76 the same way he handles Big Daddy Lipscomb of the Pittsburgh Steelers and Rosey Grier of the New York Giants.

You need an intelligent clown on a pro ball club, too, and Fuzzy is also that. He has a talent for rhyming, and when he bellows out calypso accounts of his personal heroics he doesn't need a mike.

9:02 A.M.

The players are changing into their sweatsuits in front of their dressing stalls. Their actions are leisurely and their talk the lazy talk that follows a day off. In the trainer's room Paul Hornung, in just a T-shirt and supporter, is sitting on one of the tables and Bud Jorgensen is working the diathermy over the inside of Paul's left thigh.

"How is it?" I say.

"It's pretty sore," Hornung says.

Hornung is 6-2 and weighs 215, but sitting on that table he does not look like the football player he is. His sloping shoulders are deceiving and he appears plump-bodied, but he has great underpinning. He's not as fast a starter as Jimmy Taylor but then he gets that shot of adrenalin. He has good secondary speed, a fine change of pace, has mastered that knack of working with his interference, and out in the open he has those great head, shoulder and hip feints.

"So just take it easy out there today," I say.

"I'll have to," he says.

I know he's worried. He has been worried since that afternoon in camp when Aggie kicked to him in the end zone, but last year he played our first three games with a blown-up knee and without complaining, and if it's at all possible he'll be ready on Sunday.

In the coaches' room I'm changing into a sweatsuit when Red Cochran comes in from the airport. He has the film of the opposition's game of Sunday, and Dad Braisher, our equipment manager, comes around with the lunch chart for the next two days and I order my hamburger and coffee.

"Gros won't be here today," Red says. "His wife is being operated on."

Earl Gros was our first draft choice this year, and like Jimmy Taylor, a fullback out of Louisiana State. We had him spotted as a good future prospect as early as March of his sophomore year and I remember the scout reports after that: "Excellent speed for a big man. Can cut very good. Power runner. Good receiver. . . . Size and ability is there. . . . Strong, powerful. Good hands, size, speed, quickness. Needs determination. . . . Could be a great one. Big and fast. Hasn't had desire until this year, but looks like he wants to play. . . . No defensive back. . . . Outstanding runner. Hard to bring down. Top blocker. Tough. Will get better. Great prospect."

He is out of Houma, Louisiana, and he and his wife came into town early in July with their house trailer. He had to leave right away for the All-Star camp, and his wife was ill then and had to be hospitalized. It has been tough on these two kids so far from home.

"Chuck Johnson is on the phone," Bill Austin says.

Chuck Johnson is on the *Milwaukee Journal* and he wants to check on our injuries. He knows I've seen our movies of last Sunday's game and I know he'd like me to be lavish with praise.

"I agree," I am saying. "I think we're starting to come around, but these other people are coming, too. . . . Well, they're a real fine football team. They've always had a fine defense, and now they've improved offensively, too. . . . Oh, no. I'll be satisfied to win with a field goal or a safety."

When I get off the phone Bill Austin is telling Phil Bengtson about a call he had the night before from one of the college coaches. During training camp a number of them drop in—some from as far south as Louisiana and as far west as Colorado—to observe us and, because the colleges are the spawning grounds of talent for this league, we tell them whatever they want to know about our offense or defense or our coaching methods.

"He says our option play is working great for him," Bill is saying. "And he used to hate the Packers."

"He used to hate the Packers?" Phil says.

"Yes," Bill says. "Some years ago they let one of his boys go, and I guess the kid went back and told bad stories."

That option play was one of the first things I put in when I left West Point for the Giants in 1954, and after I had spent that whole winter looking at the Giants' movies. It was in that brick split level we had just moved into in Oradell, New Jersey, and I put up the screen in the den off the kitchen. I ran that projector back and forth, night and day, until it began to drive Marie and the kids crazy and I had to take it down to the basement.

I was trying, never having played pro ball and having seen very little of it, to get a full picture of what not only the Giants but everybody in the league was doing and so I'd chart every play and every defense. On each play in every game I'd run the projector back and forth three or four times with seven or eight people in mind and then I'd run it back again to see what the three or four others were doing. I filled up those yellow legal pads and then I indexed the pads.

Frank Gifford had had only one year with the Giants then, but while he was at Southern Cal, Army had played them in the mud at the Yankee Stadium and I knew that, as a college Single-Wing tailback he had been not only a great runner but a fine passer. The optional run-or-pass play is basically a Single-Wing play, but thinking about Gifford I reasoned that we might be able to run it out of the T, but the first thing I had to do was to flank the right halfback. That gave me two men downfield—the end and the right halfback—but now I was losing that right halfback as a blocker and blocking became my problem. So I pulled the guards and either faked the fullback into the line or sent him out ahead, and it worked in New York with Gifford and here with Hornung, who was a good passer at Notre Dame.

"All right," I say now. "Let's see if they're ready out there."

Then we put in that belly play for Gifford, and this is how plays develop and how you build your offense, because what we did on the Giants was the beginning of what we do here now. That belly play was designed to go inside the left end, and our right guard, who was Bill Austin, was to pull and take the left end out. With all that emphasis inside, though, that end would pinch so hard you couldn't get him out, so Gifford, as that end would close, would dip outside of him.

This was the first time I realized that in pro ball it is to your advantage not to run to a specific hole but to run to daylight. We started to coach it and that was the beginning of that.

It was the beginning of something else, too, because we found that the defense was now so frightened of that outside threat that they were ignoring our flanker, whether it was Alex Webster or Kyle Rote, as a potential pass-receiver. That flanker was to knock the left halfback down, as Gifford faked in and ran to the outside, but in the movies we noticed that after the flanker would flatten him, the halfback would get up and make the tackle after a 6- or 7-yard gain.

We asked the flanker then to slow-block. He'd time it so that when Gifford cut to the outside he'd be throwing his block, and as a result the halfback began to come up fast on the inside and ignore the flanker. When we saw this on the films we realized that if the flanker would just fake that slow-block on the halfback and then go downfield with a burst, he'd be open. Off that belly play we had Charley Conerly fake to the fullback as usual, then fake to Gifford and throw deep down the sideline to the flanker. Charley threw at least ten touchdown passes on that one, and we're still doing it with the Packers, although we call it our 79 and have changed the backfield maneuver so that the fullback fakes up the middle instead of to the strong side, which allows the weak-side guard, rather than the strong-side guard, to pull. This gives us much better protection for the passer.

9:15 A.M.

"All right," I'm saying to them. "That was a fine performance on Sunday. They were hurt, but this was still your finest game this year. This was the first time you played a complete game without mistakes. I mean mistakes like penalties that stop us. I don't mean mistakes on plays. This is what it takes to win in this league, but you have to do it week after week. You have to knock off the contenders week after week, and you've got the big one this week."

They are in their sweatsuits, sitting on the metal folding

chairs in front of their dressing stalls or arranged in front of the screen at the end of the room. Now I want to talk about something else.

"I had a visit the other day," I say, "from two F.B.I. men and I'll tell you what they told me. They told me that they're keeping a closer watch than ever on all professional sports. The Attorney General reads every report on professional sports that comes in, and you all know what that means. You've all had this explained before, but I'll explain it again.

"There are hundreds and hundreds of thousands of dollars bet on pro football. Now you've got to be careful. If you make a phone call during which you mention that somebody on our club is hurt or in which you say what you've heard about another team you're liable to prosecution. You're liable to prosecution because they're holding that the transmission of information pertinent to gambling is the same as transporting gambling equipment.

"Now these F.B.I. men didn't mention anybody on this team, or on any other team, either, but everyone is being watched. Just imagine the result concerning not only yourself but also the Packers if one of you is picked up. Now the Commissioner tells you that every year. He comes up here and gives you an hour speech, and you've heard this before, but you've got to be careful of strangers.

"Lew Carpenter, or Jim Ringo, or any one of you, you meet a man and, if it's you, Jim, he says he's an old friend of Ben Schwartzwalder of Syracuse. He talks about his friend Ben, and what a great coach Ben is. He's a nice-looking guy and very friendly and he buys you a dinner. You mention something in the course of your conversation. It may not seem important but you mention it, and it turns out later he isn't a friend of Ben Schwartzwalder. He's never met him, and he's a hoodlum.

"What this means is that you've got to avoid all strangers. You've got to avoid them because they may be hoodlums or they may work for hoodlums, which is the same thing."

Then I give them the names of two restaurants in Chicago that the F.B.I. informed me are owned by hoodlums. One of these I was aware of before, but the other is new, and I tell them that if they are found in either of these places they are off our ball club and out of pro ball.

"And as other places crop up in other towns," I say, "I'll give you those, too."

Then we look at the movies of the Bear game. Phil and

Norb take the defense into the visitor's dressing room and I watch with Bill and Tom and Red and the offensive team.

"On your passes, Bart," I say to Starr, "you should always look at your quick man first. You'll have a quick man open first, and a slower man later."

"Yes, sir," he says, behind me in the semi-darkness.

"Our guards aren't coming out of there as they should," I am saying now as I see Jimmy Taylor stopped on our weak-side sweep after only a short gain. "The second guard—Jerry—is fine, but not Fuzzy."

"Right," Fuzzy says.

We watch Taylor score our first touchdown from the 1. The whole right side of the line blocks so well that he could have gone in from the 5, but the next time we get the ball they stop Tom Moore when their right tackle slides to his right and fills the hole.

"Fuzzy," I say, running it again, "that man is lined up on your inside. The play is going to the outside. All you have to do is shoulder block him. You knew where that play was going, didn't you?"

"It doesn't look that way," Fuzzy says.

"And, Max," I say to McGee on that pass to Ron Kramer when we score from 54 yards out, "what are you doing? You're supposed to take that man deep. You're standing around out there like a spectator!"

"I know," Max says.

We see Tom Moore hurt his shoulder and Elijah Pitts is in at left halfback. At the draft meeting for 1961 in Philadelphia they thought I was kidding when I announced, "The Packers draft Elijah Pitts from Philander Smith." I wasn't kidding, and now we watch Elijah on that option play that had its origin six years before with Frank Gifford and the Giants. He bellies his run, waits for his blockers, then runs off their blocks beautifully and goes 26 yards for a touchdown.

"How to go, Elijah!" someone hollers. They are all fond of him on the club.

"But, Elijah," Bill Austin says, "you've got to holler 'Go-go' or 'Run-run' so they know what you're going to do."

"Yes, sir," Elijah says.

The next time we run the option the Bears are looking for it and their left linebacker and left halfback come up fast. This leaves two receivers open but Elijah stays with the run, instead of passing, and they throw him for a yard loss.

44

"Don't be so quick to run," Bill Austin says. "Don't you see your receivers?"

"Yes, sir," Elijah says.

Earl Gros is in for Jimmy Taylor now and he makes 6 yards on our 36-Slant. Our left tackle does a fine job on their right end, and here I'm in trouble.

"Very good on the part of our left tackle," I say. "Who is it, Skoronski or Masters?"

"Masters," somebody says.

I know that Bob Skoronski has jersey number 76 and Norm Masters wears 78, but when I can't catch the number I can't pick between them. In my mind, as in our offense, they are interchangeable, because although Forrest Gregg is our regular right tackle, Skoronski and Masters are of such equal talent that in four seasons here I have never been able to rate one above the other.

Although they both weigh 245 pounds, what you want in your offensive tackles today is, surprisingly, not great size as much as quickness and agility. With today's defenses your offensive tackles are not blocking against the monsters, the defensive tackles, because that falls to your guards. On pass protection, however, your guards are in close quarters while your tackles have to handle and steer those defensive ends in the semi-open.

"Do you want to know something about Bob Skoronski?" Marie said to me once. "He can tell you more about the stock market than my father, and my father spent thirty years in it."

I know something else about him, too. He is high-strung, and going into a game so much emotional pressure builds up inside of him that if I do not start him he undergoes some kind of psychological relapse and he does not play up to his talent. Masters will play his game whenever you use him, and although he may suffer in the eyes of the public as a utility man he doesn't suffer in mine because on ability and desire it is a toss-up between them.

"How to go, Herb!" somebody says now.

Herb Adderley has intercepted Billy Wade's pass at midfield and with his great speed and open-field ability he goes all the way for our last touchdown. He was our first draft choice for 1961, out of Michigan State, and when I think of what he is and what he may become in our defensive backfield it scares me to remember how I almost mishandled him.

45

With his size, fine speed and open-field talent I wanted him for an offensive back. He is not one of those hard-running, driving backs, however, and although he could make a fine outside runner he didn't fit into our type of offense, and so I tried to make a flanker out of him. I was going to use his speed, and on the practice field when we found out he had good hands and was a real natural running those pass routes we thought we had it made.

Then we put him in a game, and nothing happened. He just did not look like the same ballplayer, and because he is a boy who never loosens up and who is not easy to talk with, I put old Emlen Tunnell, that great clubhouse information man, on him.

"Find out what's wrong with him," I said. "I can't figure it out."

"I'll tell you what's bothering Adderley," Emlen said a couple of days later. "He doesn't want to be a flanker. He wants to be a defensive back."

For a whole half season I had been so stubborn that I had been trying the impossible, to make something of a boy that he did not want to be, and I turned him over to Norb Hecker. We didn't use him under game conditions until Hank Gremminger was hurt and we were going into Detroit to play the Lions on Thanksgiving. I remember him on that plane going in, a first-year man and sitting alone, and then I remember him intercepting that pass when we needed it, and we beat them 17-9. On the plane coming home they were all around him and finally, and for the first time, he was a part of us.

"All right," I say, when we have gone through the whole film. "Let's get out there."

9:48 A.M.

Some of them are wearing their olive-green rain jackets over their sweatshirts and most of them have on their dark blue knitted wool skull caps. They walk in pairs or groups down the long, gentle slope of the parking area and across the concrete of Oneida Avenue, and as we get out onto the first practice field a light wind out of the north is starting to stir the morning mist and the sun, weak and brassy, is beginning to show through.

"Let's use the other field!" I shout. It cost us $19,000 just

46

to get these two fields in shape, but by using them alternately we can insure good turf. "The far field!"

"I'm sore at the coach," Bill Quinlan says to someone, but so that I can hear him.

"What's wrong with you?" I say to him.

"Your wife's giving that tea for the wives this afternoon," Quinlan says, "so I have to stay home and baby-sit."

That's my 6-3, 250-pound, ready and willing right defensive end. Out on the field, while the others are running, Jerry Kramer is skipping like a small child just let out of school. He says it loosens the ankle he broke last year.

"So how does it make you feel," a sports writer said to Jerry one day, fishing for a quote, "when you and Thurston do all the heavy work leading those plays and Hornung and Taylor get all the glory?"

"That's all right," Jerry said, in that happy way of his, "as long as they keep taking those pictures of Hornung and Taylor scoring we'll be in them somewhere."

"All right!" I shout, after they've had their ten minutes of loosening up. "Calisthenics!"

"Who leads?" someone shouts.

"Elijah! Let Elijah lead!"

Elijah Pitts, who against the Bears scored his second professional touchdown, leads them, and then we run them around the far goalposts and back and the defense splits off with Phil and Norb and the offense with Red and Bill. They go through the agility drill, on command running forward, backward, to one side or the other to further loosen those muscles dormant since Sunday, and at ten-ten I call them all together.

I am not for long practice sessions but I am for an hour or an hour and a half that is meticulously organized and intense, and this, too, is something that I got from Earl Blaik and brought away from West Point. We would arrive at that office every morning at eight and by the time we walked out onto the practice field that afternoon we would have worked out every phase and every time schedule for everything. Blaik allowed no papers on the field, so I had to have every assignment for every lineman on every play because every bit of offense and defense was given on the field, and that first spring I couldn't comprehend how you could get it all across to those cadets without a meeting. Their day was from 5:50 A.M. to 10:15 P.M. and into their minds were being crammed differential equations, the mechanics of fluids, electrical engineering, military tactics and all the rest of it. But Blaik did it.

There would be fifteen minutes to put in five plays, and I would be putting them in with the line and Paul Amen with the ends and Johnny Sauer with the backs. Then the cadet manager would blow the whistle and we'd all come together as a team and we sweated this out. The ends hadn't been with the tackles yet, but Blaik would walk into the huddle and say, "Number 10." Then we'd all stand back to see, not knowing whether they'd run together or what, and it went off like clockwork. Those cadets, as well as Blaik, were amazing. And then Blaik would say, "Number 12." I'd say, "I'm sorry, Colonel, but I didn't have time to put that play in." Then Blaik would look at me and say, "Number 14."

It was organization at its highest level. They took movies of everything, and after dinner we would be back in the office and all those pictures would be developed and waiting.

"Henry Jordan's not feeling well," Phil Bengtson is saying to me now, nodding toward Jordan, who is starting off the field. "I told him to go in and see a doctor."

So it's Tuesday, I am thinking, which is better than having him walk off the field sick on a Saturday. My first year here I traded a fourth draft choice for him and any time you can trade for one who becomes an All-Pro defensive tackle, or an All-Pro anything, that is a fortunate trade. He has a tendency to be satisfied, though, which is why I don't flatter him much and why often, when we're reviewing the pictures, I make him a target. Sometimes you will make a man a target to impress somebody else who can't accept public criticism, but I will call Hank because we both know his ability and know that I'm on him to bring it out and because he performs best when he's just a little upset.

He's a great man on tips, too, those signs an offensive man will give you now and then that indicate what he is going to do. Some of those linemen will put more weight on the front hand if they are going to drive off the ball and they will sit back a little if they are going to pass block. If a left guard is pulling right his right foot may be back slightly more than normal so that he can make that crossover step more easily. And Hank Jordan says that every now and then on a third-down-and-short-yardage situation he can tell from the guard's eyes where he is going.

Of course, the old-timers try to throw you off by using these things for their own purposes, but Hank has been around now for six years and Dave Hanner, who is in there

48

next to him, is in his eleventh season. Dave has played against these boys so long and he's so good at it that you might almost say he knows what they're going to do before they do it.

"I want to tell you something," I am saying now, and the best way I know to get them to retain this is to have them walk through it. "In a 4-3 they'll blitz 90 percent of the time."

The blitz, the sending of one or two or three linebackers across that line with the four front men, has a double defensive purpose. It is designed to get at that quarterback or to force you to keep additional personnel, your fullback or your right halfback, or both, back there to protect him instead of sending them out as receivers. What it comes down to on both sides is not just a guessing game but a contest of calculated risks in which you are both attempting to convert what you hope will be the one key equation in your favor, and on the offense an obvious answer is your series of delay plays. You've got your draw, with the quarterback dropping back but handing off to a remaining back who has faked a pass-protection block. You've got your screen, the delayed pass behind the line with the receiver led by one or more linemen. And you've got your delayed forward pass to the remaining back who blocks but then slides off to receive.

"Now your Swing Delay, your Swing-4 and your Swing-9 are all delays," I am saying to the offense. A swing pass is one on which you throw to a remaining back to the weak side, away from your flanking back. "Right, Bart?"

"Yes, sir," Starr says.

"Now give me a 4-3," I say to the defensive team. "Then give me a 6-2."

They move into their defense. I watch them come across the line, not heavy contact because they are without pads but stepping in on their blitz, and our offensive linemen enact their pass blocking and Starr throws a Swing Left to Jimmy Taylor and Taylor runs it.

"Way to go, Jimmy!" Fuzzy Thurston says.

"Now give me a Fan Wide Delay," I say to Starr, "and then a Flood Left."

"Yes, sir," he says.

A fan pass is one in which the remaining back's pass route is to the strong side, the side of the flanker. A flood pass is one in which both remaining backs, the fullback and halfback, run pass routes to the same side. After fifteen minutes of this we split them up again. Phil Bengtson and

49

Bill Austin take the defensive and offensive lines, and Bart Starr and Johnny Roach loosen their arms passing to our backs, offensive ends and flankers with the defensive backs covering them.

"All right!" I shout. "Down the other end of the field!"

For the final fifteen minutes we have our offense against our defense again, that same familiar repertoire of running plays and pass patterns. At ten-fifty-five, after the sprints, I send them in because Tuesday practice is little more than a loosening up and they've still got an hour meeting before we dismiss them and put in our toughest seven or eight hours determining exactly what, tomorrow, we are going to start giving them for this game.

11:05 A.M.

"Super Scout!" they are hollering. "Super Scout!"

They are sitting still in their sweatsuits, on the metal folding chairs distributed around the dressing room. Wally Cruice is standing at the blackboard at the stadium end of the room.

"Okay," Wally says. "I don't have to tell you how good these other people are. You know they've always been a great defensive team, and this year they've improved their offense, too. Last year their offensive tackles weren't too hot on pass blocking, but that was all you could fault them on. This year they're pass blocking well, which means they're doing everything well. Another place they've helped themselves is in their quarterback. He has taken charge and they believe in him. He's the kind who likes to throw short and control the game. He isn't as fond of the long throw, unless he's way behind or way ahead. Their 45, that halfback, has really found himself because that 23 has been pressing him hard. Their fullback, that 33, is still their big rusher. Their flanker, 41, on a Triple Left Look-in caught one for 80 yards."

He runs over all their key offensive personnel that way. He gives them the offensive statistics, team and individual, and then he goes into their formations and the plays they favor off them.

"Here's what they did off the Brown Right," he says, and he has all the plays numbered on the blackboard. "Here's their Red Right, Blue Right, Brown Left, Red Left and Blue Left. Now on this one they fake a 48, and the quarterback runs the ball on a bootlegger. He's pretty cute at it, and he may try it on you. Here are their best pass patterns. Now when they go into punt formation, they have that 28 kicking and, as you know, he handles himself pretty good back there. He not only kicks, but he passes pretty well."

He flips the blackboard over then. On the other side he has listed their defenses and in what situations they favor them against what formations.

"The 4-3 Key," he says, "is their favorite defense, and they seldom blitz their strong-side linebacker."

What this means to them now they first learned in training camp, sitting there and listening, some of them making notes in their loose-leaf playbooks, in the weeks of afternoon and evening meetings in that science building at St. Norbert. One summer we walked into the lab on the first day and there was a cat on the dissecting board, but what Wally Cruice means now is that the two enemy defensive halfbacks and safety men will key their actions to what our weak-side back, our back away from our flanker, does. If he pass blocks, their weak-side safety will go deep and play the ball. Their strong-side safety knows he is going to have that help on his inside, so he will be tough to beat with a pass to his outside and a little looser on the inside, where he'll get that help. This is just one of the almost automatic reactions on which a Key defense is based, but sometimes that weak-side safety will ignore you because he doesn't see or doesn't remember, and that can defeat you, too.

"When they're in a 6-1, though," Wally is saying, "that strong-side linebacker is going to blitz right away. They also like a regular Frisco defense and play a Man-to-Man off that. A couple of others they like are the 4-3 Zone, rotated strong, and the Safety-Up Zone. Any questions? Okay, that's all."

"Super Scout!" somebody shouts. "Super Scout!"

Then they break to take their showers and go home. Bart Starr and Johnny Roach stop Wally to ask some quarterback questions and Ron Kramer joins them with something that concerns him as our closed end.

12:15 P.M.

I have had my hamburger and coffee and take a look at Wally Cruice's scouting report. Bill Austin is setting up that portion of the film showing our opponent on defense as they beat the Colts on Sunday, and I walk into the visitors' dressing room. Phil Bengston and Norb Hecker are already screening the offensive portion.

"Did they pull both guards on that?" Phil is saying.

"Just the off guard," Norb says, meaning the guard away from the direction of the play.

"The center is blocking back," Phil says.

"The tackle is blocking down," Norb says.

"Red Right, split right end," Phil says on the next play.

"L-Turn-In," Norb says, meaning that the left end has gone straight downfield about 12 yards and made a looping turn to the inside rather than a quick hitch or a sharp hook or a 90-degree square-in. All of this, the characteristic line blocking and the pass patterns, they are noting or diagramming on those lined, yellow legal pads. I walk back to the coaches' room and Bill Austin starts the projector.

"Brown Right," he says, calling the Colts' formation.

"Frisco," Red Cochran says, calling the defense, and recording it on his pad. In the Frisco both tackles and an end shift to the strength of the offensive formation, with the middle linebacker adjusting to the weak side.

"Zone," Tom Fears says, calling the secondary pass defense.

"They'll never play us in that Zone," I say. It is the pass defense in which the three linebackers and one defensive halfback are responsible for the four short zones and the two safety men and the other halfback for the three deep ones. Theoretically all areas are covered, but there are holes between those zones so the first thing you do is send your flanker wide to one side and your split end wide to the other. This widens those holes and those are the spots your passer goes for as your receivers cut for them. You're never going to pass deep against a Zone, though, and that is why they are opening with it now against Johnny Unitas. They know he is great throwing that long ball and they don't want to give him that home run his first time up.

"They're playing this club strictly for a passing team," I say. "They've got to play us a little differently."

When I first came into this league, and after I had spent months studying those movies, it seemed to me that while the passing game was great the running game was like a half try. In those days everybody was saying that you just couldn't sustain a running game against the pros, that their defenses were too large and too mobile. They forgot that everything in football, as in physics, is relative and that the people you could put on the offense could be every bit as big and just as mobile. What they really liked about the throwing game was that only two or three key men had to be coordinated on a pass play, but a running play required the split-second timing of at least seven or eight. It is difficult not only to develop but to keep this coordination because, if you want to scrimmage once the season starts, you have to run your first offense against your first defense, and you are risking injury. What it comes down to is that to have a good running game you have to like to run as a coach. You have to derive more creative satisfaction from the planning and the polishing of the coordination of seven or eight men rather than two or three.

"We might have to fan," I say, "to get that end released."

I'm thinking of Ron Kramer, our tight end. If we fan, which means if we send Paul Hornung out in a pattern to the same side as Boyd Dowler, our wingback flanker, we will force the strongside safety to cover Paul and leave the weakside safety responsible for the whole middle-area, and both Tom Fears and I note this on our pads.

"Brown Right," Bill Austin says.

"Look how wide that weak-side safety is," I say. "I hope they play him there all day."

If he's out there against us, I am thinking, our 4-X Turn-In or 1-X Switch or 1-Zig-In might go, and I put them down as possibilities. These are combination pass plays involving both the flanker and the tight end, and we see the Colts score from 30 yards out when their wingback flies almost straight down the right side and Unitas lofts it to him.

"Maybe we ought to fly," I say to Tom Fears.

"He gave him just a little look-in," Tom says, meaning a fake to the inside. "You can't just fly on that guy."

He is talking again about that left defensive halfback, that 81. He came out of Scottsbluff Junior College and he is another one of those nobody drafted. He's the best I've ever seen.

"Look at him on this one," I say as I reverse the projector and rerun the play. The wingback has faked that fly route this time and come back and that 81 not only recovers but, at the moment the ball touches the wingback's hands, he hits him so hard he forces a fumble. "Look at that if you want to see a cat in operation."

"It makes you think," Tom Fears says, "because eleven

years ago he just walked into the Rams' camp with his newspaper clippings."

"I'm almost convinced," I say, "that we've got to throw our passes to the left side."

"Max caught fifteen against them in two games last year," Red Cochran says, referring to Max McGee, our left end, and I make a note of our turn-in and turn-out passes to Max.

"We may have something here," I say, "but I still know the only way to beat this ball club is to go out and knock their tails off. I mean on all passes they're like cats. I'm about ready to go back and look at our own pictures again to see how they defensed us and take it off that."

"On the right side," Bill Austin says, "I think our man can handle that linebacker all day. I'm not sure about the other side."

"I haven't seen one picture yet," I say, "where our tight end can't handle that guy to the inside. We ought to be able to do something with that. Let's make a note of it."

"I doubt that they'll blitz us the way they're blitzing Baltimore," Bill says, meaning they'll have more respect for our running game and for those delays we were putting in on that field a couple of hours ago.

"They didn't blitz more than twenty-six out of sixty plays," Red Cochran says, checking it in Wally Cruice's report.

"It must have been all in this second half, the way it looks," Bill says.

"All right," I say, when the film is finished. "Let's take the Blue first. They used a 4-3 Zone."

I take the sheet on which Red has listed the formations, the situations and the defenses the other people used against them. Under each I list our plays that look good against them on paper and where we may get better results varying our blocking a little, we discuss it and I diagram the plays.

"Let's see last year's cards," I say to Red finally. "Let's look at what we thought about them then."

It is something you hate to do, to repeat a game plan or lift large portions of it, for two reasons. For one, you know your opponent hasn't forgotten where and how you hurt him, but more important it makes you feel that you are losing whatever creativity you may have had. Some weeks you look at the movies of an opponent and everything falls into place, and then there are those other weeks, like this one, when the big ideas just don't come.

"It's four-forty," I say finally. "That's enough until tonight. Of course, we've got too many passes as usual. Don't put them down yet. We'll second-guess them tonight."

"Here we go again," Red says, putting our work into the big manila expansion envelopes. "I start out with ten flat folders at the first of the week, and by Tuesday they're all filled up again."

"I'm happy to report," Phil Bengston says, coming in, "that that tackle of theirs isn't as good a pass-blocker as Wally said. Marchetti was in on that quarterback all day. That's why he had to throw so quick, and they were a pretty lucky ball club."

"I hope they've run out of luck," Red says.

5:05 P.M.

Ruth McCloskey has sorted my mail and left a pile of it on my desk. I start to look through it.

Dear Coach:

I am rooting for you and I want you to be the first ever to win the National Football League title three times in a row. The main thing is you must have an excellent defense . . .

Right now I'd like to win it twice in a row, and I pick up the league statistics which include last Sunday's games. Bart Starr is fifth in passing with 57 percent completions and three touchdowns and three interceptions. The quarterback who is coming in here on Sunday leads the league with 64 percent and nine touchdowns but four interceptions. Their punter leads the league, too. But Hornung is the leading scorer and Willie Wood is first in interceptions with four. We lead in first downs rushing and rushing yardage, but they lead in total first downs and defensively. We've already had six fumbles in just three games where last year we had none at this time, but there's nothing you can do about fumbles except scream, and while statistics are interesting they're all in the past.

What it comes down to, I am thinking, is that our offensive line and running game are better than theirs. On pass defense we're about equal, but I must give them the edge in their defensive line, their kicking and their passing, and I must remember tomorrow to start relaxing Bart Starr a little if I can.

Of all the people on your ball club—and you are involved with all of them—there is no other with whom you spend as much time as you do with your quarterback. If this is a game through which you find self expression—and if it isn't you don't belong in it—then that quarterback is the primary extension of yourself and he is your greatest challenge.

"And when Vince is challenged is to try to make a great one out of a ballplayer," Marie once said, "I can only feel sorry for that player. Vince is just going to make a hole in his head and pour everything in. When it starts the player hasn't any idea what he's in for, and he hasn't got a chance. He'll get hammered and hammered until he's what Vince wants him to be. You can't resist this thing. You can't fight it. But it's more than I want to watch.

"I remember," she said, "when Susan was just starting to learn arithmetic. We'd be driving somewhere and he'd be quizzing her. 'How much is 6 plus 3? 5 plus 2? 8 minus 3? 4 plus 2?' With that persistence of his he went on and on, until I was almost out of my mind."

I know of no way but to persist, and Bart Starr with that analytic mind, retentive memory and inner toughness can take it. He is great at picking that defense apart and adjusting, and if I could just get him to be a little more daring he'd be everything. He kills them with those short ones, those singles and doubles, but he doesn't throw for those home runs often because, where Unitas or Layne or Tittle will take a chance with an offensive man and a defensive man going down the field together, he has to be sure that his offensive man has that defensive man beaten.

Your quarterback has to be stable, though, and Bart is that. I had one once who felt he was being persecuted, that his receivers were dropping the ball on purpose, and I had another who looked great throwing in practice and was letter perfect in meetings but on Sundays he couldn't find his receivers and he lost all idea of the game plan. Starr is so stable that out of the sixty-five or seventy plays we run in a game I don't send in more than ten. Then he has the right, not in the huddle but on the line, to negate anything I send in. And I'm wrong just about as often as I'm right. I remember, in fact, that season opener against this team last year and they were so inside conscious that I sent in a pitchout. They smelled it and changed their defense by looping to the outside and threw it for a 4-yard loss.

6:10 P.M.

We are having steaks, Tim Cohane and I, in Proski's, on Washington Street. Wally Proski is a brother of John Proski, the stadium manager and head groundskeeper.

"I never come out here," Cohane is saying, "without thinking of Crowley."

Jim Crowley was a Green Bay boy and one of The Four Horsemen of Notre Dame and he coached those Fordham teams, on three of which I was a 170-pound guard. He not only learned his football but also the psychology of the pep talk from Knute Rockne.

"Now remember this," Cohane is saying, imitating Crowley. "Halfway across this country, in little Green Bay, my old mother is sitting in her rocking chair by her radio waiting to hear how her son's Fordham team does on this day."

I knew he was good while I played under him, but I never knew how great he was until I got out. You have to try it yourself to really know. In my years at Fordham we never had great runners but we played two of those three consecutive scoreless ties with Jock Sutherland's Pittsburgh team that they're still calling classics. Crowley was brilliant at analyzing an offense and setting up a defense against it. When Purdue had Cecil Isbell and that great strong-side attack he overshifted two men and instead of playing in that gap between guard and tackle I ended up head-on with the end. If they had had much of a weak-side attack we'd have been dead, but we shut them out and beat them by a score I no longer remember because so many scores have gone up on that board since.

With all his brilliance he was also a precisionist. I can see him now on that Fordham Field with the wooden stands and the canvas to block off the view from the tennis courts, with the elevated structure to the west and, from the far end, that rush of passing-train noise coming up from the sunken tracks of the New York Central. He would be walking up and down the field in football pants without pads, football shoes and one of those maroon sideline hoods and wearing a baseball cap and he'd be shouting, "Blockers! Blockers! Blockers!"

If we block well here now, it began with Crowley and

with Frank Leahy, who coached that line. They drilled Nat Pierce and me on that guard-pulling action until we could do it without thinking, and there was that one day when we weren't thinking. We were in pads, but without helmets, and I pulled left and Nat pulled right and coming out of there under full steam we met behind the center. It was like a head-on car collision, and as we sat there, stunned, Crowley, who had the same disregard for small hurts that Blaik had and that I have, looked down at us and said, "Typical."

"And I remember another day," Tim Cohane is saying now. "He has made that great pre-game oration and then he stops. There's absolute silence in the room and he turns to the student manager and he says, 'Open that door and step aside. Here comes my big Fordham team.' "

6:58 P.M.

As I walk around the corner from Washington onto Crooks Street and look up I see the lights in our second-floor offices. Phil Bengston and Norb Hecker are working on their defensive charts in the outer office, and inside Bill Austin and Tom Fears and Red Cochran are waiting for me.

"All right," I say, taking off my coat. "Let's start enumerating those defenses."

These are the defenses the other people used in their two games with us last season and in their last two games this year, and we took them off those movies. There are eight defenses, but it is not quite as simple as that because in the 4-3 there's a 4-3-Inside, when the tackles drive in, a 4-3-Outside, when they drive out, a 4-3-Strong and a 4-3-Weak, in which they shift either to the strong or to the weak side of the offensive formation. In enumerating them now we list the number of times they used each defense against the various down and yardage situations—first and 10, second and long, second and short, third and long and third and short. All of this is also controlled, of course, not only by the offensive formation but by the location of the ball on the field, and all of this we must correlate before we give it to the offensive team tomorrow.

"How many times do you think they used this 4-3 on us?" I say.

"In two games?" Red says.

"Yes."

"Fifty-five times," Bill Austin says.

"Seventy-nine times," I say.

So we are going to get a lot of that 4-3. They use it more than half the time because it is basically the soundest defense against both the run and the pass. All three linebackers are in good position to move against the run quickly and to get back into their pass-defense areas, and also this other team's personnel, with their size plus agility, are perfectly suited for it.

"Now where's that Blitz Sheet?" I say, and Red Cochran gives it to me. It is a listing of the number of times they blitzed, the situation, and who did the blitzing. With the take-off of their defenses and the Blitz Sheet in front of us we look over the running plays we jotted down watching the movies yesterday and this afternoon. When we have added a few more I count them and there are twenty-one. We have in our library of running plays approximately fifty. Many of them can be run from more than one of our nine formations and, if you want to figure out the number of possible combinations this affords, you can make pro football sound as complicated as many do. Even with the pros, however, you have only so much time to put in so many plays, and so each week we limit our ready-list of running plays to about fifteen.

"I think our running game is pretty well set," I say now, "so let's look at our passes."

Again, with everything in front of us, we check the pass plays we listed in the past two days and we cut three and add two more and we have twelve. This is still too many, and we'll have to cut again.

"What else do we want to do from the Double-Wing?" I say. We are putting in the Double-Wing this week because we feel that whenever we use it we will force the weak-side safety to stay honest. We feel he must honor the man in the slot, the left halfback, rather than just play as a free safety.

Norb Hecker has come in and, at the duplicating machine, he has been running off for the defensive team copies of the scout report expanded by what he and Phil Bengston picked up from the films. Then he runs off the frequency chart, covering everything that the other people have run, where they ran it and how often. When he finishes, Bill Austin runs off copies of the offensive pass blocking against the various defenses and then the diagrams of the twenty-one running plays and the twelve pass plays for this week.

While they are doing that I'm drawing up the charts of the other people's defenses, how many times they have used them and how many times against us, each defense on an 8 by 11 white cardboard.

I'd hate to put in a play where we haven't got a chance of protecting ourselves, I am thinking, looking at the Blitz Sheet again, but if they blitz us there will be those times when they're wide open. I am thinking of, in addition to our delay plays, a play in which we divide our backs, split them on a pass pattern, but I decide it is not worth the risk of leaving Bart Starr back there without that protection.

"Have they got a lot of offense, Phil?" I say, seeing Bengtson come in from the other office.

"A variety of stuff," he says. "Brown, Red, Green, Double-Wing."

"We're putting in a little ourselves," I say, and I am wondering if there isn't something we have overlooked. I am fighting that urge to put in just one or two more, trying to convince myself that this is all we will need, because tomorrow we must start to convince all of them.

It is ten-twenty when we leave and, driving home, I see again the lights of the paper company across the river and reflected in the water.

WEDNESDAY

7:45 A.M.

Marie is running a fever now, so this Spartan business of ignoring the small hurts has gone far enough. I finally talk her into calling the doctor and I wait in the car while Susan rounds up her books and her homework.

It has been raining during the night and the trees are still dripping water and the streets are strewn with wet leaves. It is one of those times when the air is so gray-blue and heavy with moisture that you cannot understand why it is not raining.

"Don't forget me," Susan says.

I drop her at the corner and then have to wait again for that traffic light. On our sweep, I am thinking, we ought to be able to do something if our tight end, fullback and right tackle can recognize on the field the difference between that 4-3 and the 6-1 defense. It looks easy on paper and on the film, but when they line up against you they actually appear the same. The difference is that in the 6-1 the linebackers blitz and the defensive end plays it a lot tighter over our tackle. This stops our tackle from releasing and taking the middle linebacker and leaves that 56 without a blocker on him. Therefore if we can recognize the 6-1 and change our assignments so that the tackle will hook the end and our tight end will release and take the middle linebacker and our fullback will handle the blitzing linebacker, that sweep should pour around that end. This involves three men, though, and their instant recognition of that 6-1 on the snap of the ball.

8:31 A.M.

When I come out of St. Willebrord's it has started to mist, and by the time I get to Sneezer's it is raining hard. We can put in our running game rain or not, but in this kind of weather we're in trouble with our passing game. I pick up a copy of the *Milwaukee Sentinel* and sit down at the counter.

Bud Lea's thesis is that we're not a gambling team and that our opponent is. As far as I can make out he arrives at this conclusion because last Sunday, late in the game, on the Bears' 47-yard line with fourth down and a yard to go and leading by 42-0, we kicked. At Baltimore, with less than a yard to go on the Colts' 45-yard line, the other people tried a quarterback sneak that went all the way. The difference, of course, is that the other people were losing at the time and we were ahead six touchdowns. We're not sadists and our defensive team wanted a shutout.

"We'll beat the Packers," he quotes one of their tackles as saying, "if we have to take guns and knives with us."

I like that. It brightens my day just a little because, week after week, you have to scratch to find some way to keep your own people emotionally up, and this can be a help.

9:02 A.M.

It is still raining hard when I get to the stadium. I see two empty buses are parked there. They must have brought one of the high school bands to practice on the field. When I get out of the car I can hear them practicing under the stands.

"Henry Jordan is pretty sick with the flu," Phil Bengtson tells me. "The doctor's keeping him home today."

Great, I'm thinking. We may get rained out of this practice and Hank Jordan has the flu. How lucky can we get?

"You see the paper?" Norb Hecker says. "They're going to beat us if they have to use guns and knives to do it."

"I saw it," Bill Austin says. "If we win this week, how are we going to get them up for next week?"

"I'm not worried about that," I say. "How about calling the airport for the weather report?"

Dad Braisher, our equipment manager, comes around with the lunch chart and I order my hamburger. I look at a copy of the opponents' pass routes that Phil and Norb have taken off the films.

"General rain all day," Bill says, hanging up the phone. "Possible let-up late this afternoon. Tomorrow clear."

"In Virginia," Dick Voris is saying, "they learn Virginia history before they learn United States history."

In addition to being our personnel director he does some coaching of our ends. He was line coach of the Rams and put in three years with Earl Blaik at West Point, and he was head coach at the University of Virginia when I got him last year.

"That's like it is here," Norb Hecker says. "In the first grade they learn the Packer fight song at the same time as they learn *The Star-Spangled Banner*."

"All right," I say. "Let's get them organized out there. We'll have our meeting now."

They are sitting around in their sweatclothes in front of their dressing stalls. Red Cochran sets up the screen and Bill Austin brings out the opaque projector and those 8 x 11 white cardboard charts we made up last night.

"We'll have our meeting now," I say to them, "and then take a look at the weather. To begin with, maybe you don't realize it, but these other people are talking a great game. They're high and mighty. You know they've been saying that they're not so sure they can beat the Giants but that they know they can beat us. Now they're saying that they'll beat us if they have to use guns and knives to do it.

"Now this is a great challenge, gentlemen. It's a great challenge and I'm looking forward to it. This is going to be a real football game, the kind I like. They're a fine football team and they're going to make a great effort and it's going to take a great effort on your part to beat them. I'm sure you're looking forward to it as I am. It's our opportunity to knock off a big contender, and we've got to knock them off this Sunday."

This is not easy, this effort, day after day, week after week, to keep them up, but it is essential. Each week there is a different challenge, but there is also that unavoidable degree of sameness to these meetings.

Now the defensive team has filed into the other dressing room. For the offense Bill Austin is projecting onto the screen the chart of the defenses the other people use, the number of times they used each in those first-and-10, second-and-long, second-and-short, third-and-long and third-and-short situations.

"You will notice," I say, "that only fifteen times in four ball games were they confronted with a third-and-short situation. You know what that means. It means that they're a fine defensive ball club, and fourteen out of those fifteen times they used a 6-1. As you can also see, the 4-3, Frisco and 6-1 are their major defenses. Have you got that all down, Bart?"

"Yes, sir," Starr says.

"Now the middle linebacker, this 56, is very quick and very fast and he's everything they say he is. This left linebacker, this 57, will try anything he can. He's a rough customer, so remember that, Ron."

"Right," Ron Kramer says.

"Now I don't want any nonsense out there," I say to him, because he tends to flare up and I remember one day when, right out in the open, he kicked a linebacker on the shin and cost us 15 yards. "We can't afford to lose a man and we don't want penalties. If he starts some of this foolishness with you, just tell the official."

"Right," Ron Kramer says.

"Now about their blitzes," I say as Bill Austin projects the Blitz Sheet, the black lines for the normal rush and the blitz paths in red. "They blitz all the time, regardless of the down and yardage, and in all combinations."

"They only blitzed one out of eleven on third down and long this year," Red Cochran says.

"That surprises me," I say. "And Jerry?"

"Here," Jerry Kramer says.

"This 71 likes to come to the inside. Remember that, but

don't hop to the inside or he'll jump outside. He's quick, so let him come to the inside and handle him there."

"Yes, sir."

"On their pass coverage," I say, Bill has that chart up there now, "remember this left halfback, this 81, is dangerous on a turn-in. He gets in front of you, and remember again that even when he makes a mistake he recovers well. The middle linebacker, that 56, is devoted to the fullback. That's their key, and only in the Zone, which they used only 19 times in four ball games, does he go away from the fullback.

"Now remember this. Their 6-1 is a storm, and they used it forty-two times, fourteen against us in two games. Your best play against this is your weak-side sweep. Their 6-2 they used against us only twice, but this year they've used it seventeen times. And one other thing about their blitzes: they're in there on first down and 10 to upset you. They want to get two and long and then they'll do it again to get three and long. This is their pattern, because all well-coached clubs have patterns and this is a well-coached club."

Bill Austin takes the offensive line into the coaches' room and the backs and receivers stay with Red Cochran and Tom Fears. I check on the defensive team, and when I come back Red is projecting the listings of the running plays and pass plays, one chart for those to the right and one for the left, the plays listed in the color—red, brown, blue—of the formation from which they will be used. Then he turns on the light and diagrams backfield blocking, on which there is a question.

"On this one, Max," I say to Max McGee, citing our Flood pass, "you know you're not going to get the ball, but you must make that safety man as well as the halfback cover you. Give that halfback a feint outside, and then go in and make it sincere. If this is going to work you've got to make the safety cover you."

If Max were a perfectionist there is no telling how great a receiver he might be, but then, pressing all the time as perfectionists must, he would probably lose one of his greatest assets, his ability to relax. He can relax before, during and after a game, and it makes him a great clutch player, although it also contributes to his tendency to be a little careless. He has great deception, great moves, but if he is not going to get that ball, as on that crossing pass that Ron Kramer caught against the Bears on Sunday, he may not take that halfback or safety man or both with him the way he should. Then I've seen him drop the easy pass and make the great one-hander. All receivers will do that, of course, but Max more than most.

"Right, coach," he says now.

He is 6-2 and 205 pounds and at the age of 30 he is a mature, attractive guy to whom material gain means a great deal. As Marie says, there is an air of mystery about Max and he tends toward cynicism. He is highly intelligent, with a sardonic sense of humor, and they tell of the time when one of the Packers borrowed Max's new car and the police called him to tell him that it was parked in the front window of a downtown department store.

"So how much furniture have we bought?" Max said.

Then there was the time Max caught one of those hair-raising one-handers of his in the end zone. It was on an option play pass from his buddy, Paul Hornung, and a sports writer asked him about it.

"Hornung is supposed to make me look good on those," Max said. "On that one he made me look ridiculous."

As relaxed as he is, Max is not without nerves, of course, but the really mature ballplayer is the one who has learned to conquer them. When the Packers drafted Max from Tulane in 1954 he was a halfback but they converted him to an end immediately. He says that, like almost all young receivers in this league, he was gun-shy at first on that slant over the line where, reaching for the ball, you are an open target.

"Billy Howton had had a couple of years of it by then," Max says, "and he told me, 'Look. You might as well catch it because they're going to knock the hell out of you anyway.' Then Bobby Mann was a nine-year vet and he taught me his moves, so they cut him."

In Max's first year the Lions were defending champions. Max was sitting with Dave Hanner on the bus to the ball-park to play them.

"Hanner told me about a dream he had the night before," Max says. "He said, 'Max, I dreamt there were ten seconds to go and you were alone in the end zone and you dropped the ball.' With fifteen seconds to go I went down and in. I was in the end zone alone so, to fulfill Hanner's dream, I dropped the ball and blew the game. Hanner will never forget it."

I keep after Max about that tendency toward carelessness, because I know it's not laziness—he'll run from the moment he gets on that practice field. His courage goes beyond extending for the catch, too, because I remember when he played with those cracked ribs and they had no sooner healed when they were cracked a second time. Bud Jorgensen put a pad on them and Max went right out there again.

"Any time you see this man here," I am saying now, meaning the opponent's outside linebacker, who is playing close to his end, "you've got to play him from the near position."

We have three positions for our offensive ends. In the regular position he splits three yards from the tackle, in the near position he is out 6 to 8 yards and in the far position he is out anywhere beyond those 8 yards. The play also dictates where our flanker sets, and the positions for both of them are established for each play each week, depending on the opponent. In any of the formations from which our plays are run the end may be in any one of three positions and the flanker may be outside or inside the end, making it, in effect, a different formation.

"Have you got that, Gary?" I say.

Gary Barnes was our third draft choice this year, 6-4, 210 pounds and out of Clemson. He is one of the four first-year men who survived out of the twenty-four we brought to camp.

"Yes, sir," he says.

"How far is the near position?" I say.

He hesitates. There is so much they must learn in their first year, but certainly he must know this. I'm sure he knows it, but that first year unsettles a lot of them and until they begin to feel secure they can't acquire poise. If he hesitates here, though, he will hesitate on that field, and they can acquire some of that security, some of that poise, right here.

"Well," he says now, "6 to 8 yards."

"Right!" I say, and when the rest of them laugh I laugh with them, and Barnes grins. "6 to 8 yards. You're right, Gary."

"How to go, Gary!" somebody says.

"Someone open that door and look at the weather."

"It's not raining now," Ron Kramer says when he comes back, "but it looks like it might start again."

"Okay," I say. "Let's go down."

11:35 A.M.

"Stay off the fields!" I am hollering. "Run in the middle!" Walking on that turf is like walking on sponges. They have their hooded rain jackets on over their sweat clothes and their dark blue stocking caps and some of them have towels around their necks.

At the green ball bag, at the foot of the pipe tower that stands between the two fields for the photographers and cameramen, Bart Starr is trying to find a passing ball. Over a period of time an inflated football will swell a little. I don't mean that it will ever become as corpulent as those we used in the Thirties, but the quarterbacks know the difference, and this is as good a moment as any for me to try to relax Starr a little.

"How are you today, Bart?" I say.

"Fine, coach."

"You had a real fine day on Sunday."

"Thank you, sir," he says.

"You were a little tense in that first quarter."

"I know."

"There's no reason for that. You don't have to feel week after week that you're carrying the whole burden of this ball club on your shoulders."

"I know," he says, "but I do get a little tense."

"Relax. You just do your job—and you're doing a great job—and the others will do theirs. Just go out there and run that club and throw that ball."

"Yes, sir," he says. "I understand."

"All right!" I say, shouting it. "Calisthenics! Let's go! Let's go!"

We are all breathing moisture and we will have to hurry if we are going to get much in today. Overhead the low clouds are closing down on us, scudding from east to west, but when I look back toward the stadium I see the higher clouds, black, moving in from the west. We are going to have to hurry because there isn't much time, but there's never enough time and we are hurrying from the day that camp opens in mid-July until the end of December, if we make the championship playoff again.

I remember that afternoon last summer when Bill Austin, with that private pilot's weather eye of his, spotted that electrical storm coming from over beyond the stadium. It was the third week in July, but there was so little time even then that we brought the two yellow school buses we use to get the team from St. Norbert to here and back, down from the stadium to the field. When the rain started we kept right on working but when the lightning began to hit around us we ran into the buses. When it let up a little we ran out again to get in another ten minutes before we had to quit, and there must have been a thousand people who sat it out through that rain and lightning in those bleachers along Oneida Avenue while we were in the buses.

Then there was the afternoon two years ago when that rain and windstorm hit and Ray Nitschke walked over to that 15-foot-high camera tower to find his helmet. He had just put it on when the wind toppled the tower and it fell on Nitschke and knocked him to the ground. When he got up there was a hole in his helmet where one of the tower bolts had gone right through it. If he had not had the helmet on it would have gone right into his skull, but he just got up with a big grin on his face—that's Ray Nitschke.

"All right!" I shout. "Around the goalposts! Let's go!"

Ray Nitschke is the rowdy of this team and the whipping boy because he needs it and he can take it. He has the proper temperament for a middle linebacker, but maybe too much of it. He is a big, 6-3 235-pound, rough, belligerent, fun-loving guy with a heart as big as all outdoors, but he's been a problem to coach. When you chew him out he's like a child. He's repentant and never gives you an argument, but then he turns around and does the same thing over again, and one of the best things that ever happened for Nitschke and this ball club is his marriage. It has settled him down. Criticism still rolls off him until you wonder if it helps him at all. You don't improve him, but happily he improves himself. The Packers drafted Nitschke as a fullback from Illinois. When they shifted him to linebacker it delighted him, because on defense you can use your hands before other people can get to you, and he says that he has enjoyed belting other people since he was a kid growing up in a suburb of Chicago.

"My father died when I was three," he said once, "and my mother when I was fourteen, so I took it out on all the other kids in the neighborhood. That's what I like about this game—the contact, the man-to-man, and you get it out of your system."

"I'm not that way at all," Dan Currie said, listening to him. He's our left linebacker. "I like the scientific, the artistic side. I mean I like the feeling you get when you make the good, clean, perfect tackle. With me it's the tackle instead of just belting the other guy."

"Not with me," Nitschke said.

Currie is 6-3 and 240 and he was an All-American center

68

and linebacker at Michigan State and the Packers' first draft choice in 1958. Where criticism just bounces off Nitschke it cuts so deep into Currie that I have to be careful. My first year here I read him out in front of the others just once and I knew immediately that he resented it and that it wouldn't help. Even in private you have to be careful how you handle him, but if you tell him he's playing well he'll go out there and kill himself for you.

"Dan Currie," Marie said once, "could be a bank president some day. He could set the world on fire if he only had the desire to do it."

They're a great pair, Nitschke and Dapper Dan, against that strong-side stuff. Nitschke has that raucous, flat voice, and when those other guards pull and that cavalry charge starts toward them you can hear him across the field: "Dapper! Dapper! Look out, Dapper! Here they come!"

Phil Bengtson takes the defensive line now and Bill Austin the offensive line. The rest of them line up in two rows for the passing drill.

"Let's keep the balls dry!" somebody shouts. "Nobody drop it!"

Nobody does. They go downfield, one from one row and then one from the other, and Bart Starr and Johnny Roach, alternating, throw to them. They have thrown maybe two dozen before Johnny leads Elijah Pitts by just a little too much, and Elijah juggles it and drops it and the others boo him and razz him.

"All right!" I say. "Let's go to our pass plays. C'mon! C'mon!"

The rain has started again now and we are going to have to hustle to get everything in. We start on the twelve pass plays we have settled on in those two days and nights of watching movies. We work against our linebackers and the defensive backfield, with the linebackers stepping through those blitz patterns we have taken off the screen.

"Defense, here!" I shout, after about ten minutes of it. It is raining harder now. "Let's get that defense over here!"

We work on the running plays, the first of the twenty-one we have put in, and it is raining so hard now that John Gordon, our clubhouse boy, has to work with the towel to keep the balls we alternate dry. As we go into our various formations Ray Nitschke, backing that middle line, calls them for the defense.

"Double-Wing!" he is shouting. "Double-Wing!"

"Not so loud," I say, and on the following play I watch them fake our 49 and Ron Kramer come around from right end and take the ball on a reverse.

I look across the field and there is one man in the bleachers. He is standing there watching us with his raincoat over his head.

"Who's that guy?" I say to John Gordon. "Only a nut would stay out in a rain like this unless he's scouting. Find out who he is."

I don't make a fetish of secrecy. I mean I don't hold secret practice or burn the contents of our wastebaskets every night, but if it comes as news to the other people the first time we go into that Double-Wing we may pick up some extra change.

"He's a salesman from Sheboygan," John Gordon says when he comes back. Then he shows me a business card. "He says he's a Packer fan and, as long as he was in town, he wanted to see them."

It's possible. In fact, if in this town they teach the Packer fight song with *The Star-Spangled Banner* and if a thousand of them will sit through a summer lightning storm just to watch us sit in buses, it's possible, and I'd be the last one to discourage it.

"Taylor!" Red Cochran is hollering now. And Jimmy, who has been talking with Max McGee, turns and comes trotting back. "Why do you always have to be off visitin' with somebody?"

"Well," Jimmy says, "he asked me a question."

It is typical of Jimmy, who always hates to admit he's wrong and has to justify himself in front of the others. His justification, of course, is when he carries that ball. Now Starr calls our 36, our fullback slant, and Jimmy bursts out of there like he has been shot from a cannon. He makes his cut to the left. There was a time when, almost inevitably, he would cut to the right. He loved to plant that left foot hard and push off it, but Red finally got him out of it and he's as good going to the left now as to the right.

"Tom!" I shout to Tom Moore. "On that sweep you go outside—outside of Fuzzy!"

It began to be a part of me, this sweep, this pay-off-the-mortgage play they are now calling The Lombardi Sweep, during my days at Fordham. I was impressed playing against the Single-Wing sweep the way those Pittsburgh teams of Jock Sutherland ran it. And I was impressed again in those early days of attending coaching clinics when the Single-

Wing was discussed. Today our sweep has a lot of those Sutherland qualities, the same guard-pulling techniques, the same ball-carrier cutback feature, and there's nothing spectacular about it. It's just a yard-gainer, and I've diagrammed it so many times and coached it so much and watched it evolve so often since I first put it in with the Giants eight years ago that I think I see it in my sleep.

And I can hear myself at that blackboard, over and over:

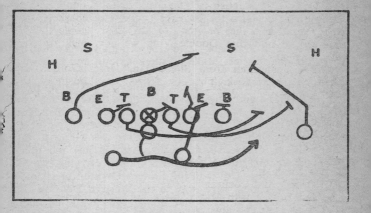

"Right end—drive that man over you in the direction of his angle. Never allow penetration to the inside or over you hard. If he penetrates inside he knocks off both our pulling guards. Your eyes and your weight should be to the inside. If he comes to the inside he takes a big gamble. If he goes to the outside you set and don't make your move until he's past your nose and then drive—drive—drive him to the sideline.

"Right tackle and fullback—you work as a unit, responsible for the left end and middle linebacker. For a sweep to be successful you can't have penetration by the defensive end. Tackle—drive the end unless he's outside you. If he's outside, slam, and set yourself up in the seal position and seal inside. Fullback—drive the first man outside your tackle, and you can't make a curved or circle approach to that man. Speed is absolutely necessary for the first guard, the onside guard, to clear. If none outside your tackle, if the tackle has taken him, seal inside for the middle linebacker.

"First guard—the onside right guard must pull hard to

clear the fullback's move. Ninety-five percent of the time you will pull outside your onside end. Center—cut off that left tackle onside, because he'll have nobody over him. This is one of the two toughest blocks involved, but you must make it. Second guard—the offside left guard must pull hard, look for the hole and seal to the inside. Offside tackle —the left tackle must cut off the defensive right tackle. He'll also have nobody over him and you must pull like a guard. This is the second of the two toughest blocks, because you must take him where you find him, whether he comes across that line or whether he slides with the play. You must block him. Flanker—take the left safety man, wherever he is. Halfback—come hard until you get that ball from the quarterback. Make a little belly-out, and then wing! That's it."

That's it, but that left tackle, pulling, doesn't know where his man will be and either Skoronski or Masters has his work cut out for him. Not every center can perform that block like Jim Ringo, and when Ernie Stautner was a great defensive tackle* with the Steelers no center was going to take him with an onside block because he was just too quick. With the Giants, though, and with Gifford carrying, we had that great success with it in the Eastern Division in 1956-57-58 and it was great here, too, in the Western Division with Hornung carrying in 1959 and '60. In 1961 it started falling off a little as play recognition by the defense began to develop, but in that 1961 championship playoff against the Giants Hornung made one 19-yard gain with it. Then the Giants adjusted and when they drove Jim Katcavage, their left end, upfield hard, we used the counter. We ran inside instead of outside, using cross-blocking, because a play's value is not only in that play itself but in the counter it sets up.

"All right!" I say now. "That's all."

It is twelve-thirty and raining harder, and I send them in. On the way off the field I join up with Hornung. I can tell from the hang of his head that he's depressed.

"How's it feel?" I say.

"It's still sore," he says.

"So just take it easy," I say. "You can't hurry it."

"I know," he says.

Ahead of us I see Earl Gros. With everything else, I have forgotten to ask about his wife.

* Stautner now plays defensive end for Pittsburgh.

72

"She's all right," he says. "Thank you."

"The operation went all right?"

"Yes, sir. That's what the doctor said."

"That's fine."

Behind me Jimmy Taylor is talking to someone.

"I used to like to deliver papers on a day like this," he says. "I mean in the rain—when I was a kid."

"Why?" the other says.

"It used to make me feel good," Jimmy says. "You know, through the rain and tryin' to throw them in a puddle."

"Where would you throw them on a nice day?"

"Up on the porch roof," Jimmy says, "or you'd try to knock over the milk bottles."

1:30 P.M.

They have had almost an hour to shower and have their lunch, and now Phil and Norb have the defense in the other room and Bill and Tom and Red and I have the offense again. We are showing them the opposition's game of last Sunday against the Colts, stopping the projector and running it back again and again so that they will know the reasoning behind our thinking, behind what we are putting in for this game and what we are asking them to do.

They call it coaching, but it is teaching. You do not just tell them it is so, but you show them the reasons why it is so and you repeat and repeat until they are convinced, until they know. It was the way, back in Brooklyn, the good teachers I had and admired did it—Father Smith and Father McGoldrick, teaching Latin at Cathedral Prep, and Danny Kerr in English at St. Francis Prep, and Harry Kane coaching us. We'd dress for practice at the school but have to bus from Butler Street to the Todd shipyard across the East River from the skyscrapers of Manhattan. It was a storage lot with no grass on the field but pieces of iron lying around, and Harry Kane, short and gray-haired and with that high-pitched voice, had everything set in a pattern. It was so many steps out or over and then in, and he made the reasons clear.

I admired them all, the good teachers as well as the good coaches, and the good students as well as the good athletes, and the truth is, when Marie and I decided to get married and I quit Fordham Law after two years, I believe I wanted to be a teacher more than a coach. At St. Cecilia they had me

73

teaching physics, chemistry and Latin, as well as coaching baseball, basketball and football with Andy Palau. And that first year, before I got my courses set, it was like it is every year in this game. In each course it was a case of keeping one lesson ahead of the class, which is what we have to do here, week after week and game after game.

"Our 24 ought to be a good one," I am saying to them now. On the screen we have seen our opponent shift to a Frisco defense, in which they overshift the two tackles and the end toward our flanker. Therefore our weak-side play, 24, hitting inside the end away from the overshift and with cross-blocking technique, should be a good one.

"The end releases and takes the middle linebacker," I say, "and brother, we should clean them up."

Andy Palau was our 160-pound quarterback at Fordham, courageous, intelligent, serious and a worrier, and before that first season at St. Cecilia he and I had those big meetings about what we would use. We ended up, of course, using the old Notre Dame Box, lining up in the T and shifting into the Box: the quarterback shifting to outside the right guard, the right halfback to wingback outside the right end, the fullback behind the right tackle and the left halfback behind the center. We ended up using it because it was what Crowley had given us at Fordham and it was all we really knew. And in this coaching business, as in anything else, that's where you have to start.

After playing in college, the first time I saw those high school kids on that practice field in MacKay Park they looked like babies to me. Now when our college draftees first turn up in camp they are the ones who look like babies. In that first year at St. Cecilia we naturally made the same mistake everyone does. We tried to give them too much. To run through everything we would have had to have stayed out there seven hours, but this was my first experience in giving rather than receiving. It was the first time, too, that I truly realized that a ball club is made up of as many different individuals as there are positions on it, that some need a whip and others a pat on the back, and others are better off when they are ignored, and that there are limitations imposed by the difference in physical ability and mentality. The amount that can be consumed and executed by a team is controlled by the weakest man on it, and while others can give him physical help, he has to do his own thinking.

74

I remember one practice when we were running one play, a reverse, over and over and our end was making the same mistake over and over. Finally he got so frustrated that he cried, and I realized then that he was just a seventeen-year-old kid and we were asking the impossible.

It has happened here, too. One year here our fourth draft pick was a 6-1, 240-pound lineman who had a great playing record in a tough college league. He was an A student in one of the sciences, with a fine mind and physical toughness, but he broke down mentally in every game and even in practice.

You could go through his playbook with him and he'd never bust an assignment, but he'd bust them on the field. In private sessions he'd be perfect, but on the field he'd break down. You don't have to be a genius to play this game, but we do a lot of changing on the line of scrimmage—those check-offs, the calling of automatics—and he just couldn't pick it up. He simply did not have a football mentality.

"Can you tell me what's the matter?" I said to him one day.

"I don't know," he said, hanging his head. "I just don't know."

We used him in spots, but he wouldn't pull when he was supposed to pull, or he'd block the wrong man, and the end came when we had him in once against Detroit. From the sideline I saw big Alex Karras barrel in and almost kill Bart Starr. I thought it was the end of my team. I knew something went wrong, but I thought maybe Karras had just defeated my man until, the next morning, we saw the pictures. Starr had converted from a running play to a pass play and my friend had pulled, instead of pass blocking.

Our system of calling the change-up—the check-off, the automatic—on the line of scrimmage is simple enough so that an A student, or a C student, should be able to get it eventually. In the huddle Starr will say, "34 on 3." The "34" is the play number and the "3" is the snap number. On the line of scrimmage, if the play stands, he will call "Set!" two numbers that are meaningless and then "Hut! Hut! Hut!" On the third "Hut!" Jim Ringo snaps the ball and they go. If Starr decides, on the line, to convert to another play from 34 on 3 he will call "Set! Three!" and then the new play number. The repetition of the snap number, the "3," means that a change-up is coming, but the opponent is unable to tell whether the play number is real or not because he doesn't know what snap number was set in the huddle. In scrimmage even our own defense, which knows all our plays and their numbering, is guessing.

"What was he doing?" I said to Bill Austin then, and I was still hurting from the way Karras, with no one in front of him, had boomed in and dropped his 270 pounds on Starr.

"He was pulling," Bill said.

"I'm sorry," I said, "but he's gone."

Now we have run through the film and it is two-thirty-eight. I send the players home. Bill Austin is carrying the projector into the coaches' room.

"They didn't look so tough that time," he says. "It's like a horror movie. The second time you see it, it doesn't scare you half as much."

I start cutting some of the plays we have listed, and then, while I take a shower, Bill and Red Cochran go over the film of our Bears game of Sunday once more. Red takes off the Bears' defenses on each play, the yardage we made and who made the tackle, and Bill starts grading our players for what you might call our Honors Assembly after practice on Friday.

The key to grading players is the recognition of the fact that some positions are more difficult to play than others. On pass plays, for example, your center and your guards and tackles should make 85 percent of their blocks for a passing grade, while your ends have no blocking responsibility. On running plays 55 percent is a passing grade for your split end, 60 percent qualifies your center, guards, and tight end, while your tackles should make 65 percent. The percentages for backs are 60 percent on runs and 85 percent on passes, and anyone who hits his percentages on both running and passing wins acclaim. You grade your defensive backs on a plus-and-minus point system, and an interception helps a score the most. On a good day a defensive back will break even, and a plus score means he played an unusually fine game.

3:45 P.M.

I have been sitting at my desk in the office for about twenty minutes, going through the mail, when I come to this one:

76

Dear Mr. Lombardi:

I will pass on to you the following observation regarding rushing the passer. When rushing the passer, the first man in may throw a fast, sweeping block. The passer is blind, so to speak, to the low approach off a fast block. Caution: do not have your own men try out this technique on your passer or passers, for you may hurt these good men. If you happen to block the passer as he plants his feet to throw it's all over for him as an effective passer.

Now, if you will sit right down and go over the film of your game with the Vikings . . .

Instead of sitting right down and going over the film of our game with the Vikings I will go home and see how Marie is feeling and if there is anything I can do for her.

5:30 P.M.

Marie is still running a temperature but the doctor has given her something and there is nothing I can do. If she misses this game it will be, I think, the first home game she has missed in my twenty-four years of coaching, so I'm betting she'll make it.

I shave and put on a blue shirt and drive through the rain to the studios of WBAY-TV. They are in an imposing former school building on Jefferson Street, and although this is the third Wednesday I have been coming here for what they call *The Vince Lombardi Show*, I get lost again before I find Dave Barnhizer, the producer, and Don Hutson. Don has a thriving automobile agency now in Racine, Wisconsin, and he does not look much heavier than he did when, from 1935 through 1945, he racked up those 105 touchdowns and was the greatest pass-receiving end this game has known.

"Am I supposed to be able to read this?" I say.

The producer has handed me a copy of the script, but someone has made one too many copies and mine is faint and fuzzy. I'll never be able to read it.

"We have a new girl in the office," the producer says, "and she must have been sleepy or something. It's going on the Tele-PrompTer, anyway."

"Why sure, Vincent," Don Hutson says in that easy, affable way of his, because he has the ability to relax that all great receivers, or performers, must have. "We'll be great tonight."

"*You* may be," I say.

Red Cochran comes in and we go upstairs for the first run-through against Al Sampson's film of those plays Tom Miller and I picked on Monday morning out of the play-by-play of our Bears game. Red Cochran will read off the situation and I will read the description of the play.

"Vince," the producer says, "put down cue line—'second quarter.'"

So on my copy, which I can barely read, I put down the cue line "second quarter" and Red says, "First and 10 on the Packer 34." I say, "Taylor gains 7 on a slant off left tackle." Then Red says and I say and Red says and I say until Taylor scores our first touchdown.

"Now we have a commercial," the producer says.

We run through all the key play sequences that way. We are ahead 42-0 and not really looking for any more when Herb Adderley intercepts that pass and busts fifty yards for the final score.

"Good," the producer says. "Don't worry about a thing. It'll all iron out."

Would he like to bet? When we drafted Adderley as our first choice for 1961 he was to play in the Shrine Game and we sent Bill Austin right out to San Francisco to sign him. He found Herb in the locker room at Santa Clara University, where the East team was training, but he also found one of the coaches from the Canadian league with him. The Canadian coach was hollering that Bill should be thrown out and Bill was hollering that the Canadian coach should be thrown out and the three of them ended up in the parking lot with Bill hanging onto one of Adderley's arms and the Canadian coach the other. Then the Canadian coach swung at Bill and Bill swung at him and finally Bill said, "Herb, it's up to you. Here's your bonus check. All you have to do is sign this contract." Adderley signed it on the hood of a car, and then I spent all those weeks trying to make a receiver out of him before I found out he wanted to be, and was meant to be, a defensive back.

"Now we have this film of Hornung demonstrating kicking the extra point with Starr," the producer says.

Paul does typically well. He explains that Bart Starr marks, with the extended fingers of his left hand, the point 7 yards from the center, where he will place the ball. Paul starts moving as soon as the ball reaches Bart's hands and, while

Bart is turning the ball so the laces are forward and placing it, Paul is making the two steps it takes him to reach and kick the ball.

"And now," he says, in the Hornung manner, "I turn you back to my special guests—Vince Lombardi and Don Hutson."

"If you don't look out," Red Cochran says, "this will end up as Hornung's show."

"Then, Vince, you diagram that pass play," the producer says, "and then you and Don talk about next Sunday and it'll be fine."

Sure it will be fine, and we go downstairs to the set and I eat my second hamburger of the day off the top of a grand piano. It is seven o'clock and we still have to go through one more rehearsal before we go on at eight o'clock, and then Red and I have to get back to the office because we still have to put in our goal-line plays for Sunday. What day is it now?

We use a study set, with a false fireplace and three chairs and a coffee table in front of it. The announcer introduces Don and me and I introduce Red and we run through it this time with the TelePrompTer until we are ready to go into the fourth quarter. Then, although I can't see them, I can hear the voices of Ray Nitschke and Henry Jordan paying tribute to a gasoline.

When we have finished the fourth quarter I get up to go to the board to diagram the crossing pattern on which Ron Kramer caught a pass and went 54 yards for a touchdown, and I trip over the cord of the lavalier mike around my neck. I show how Max McGee draws that defensive man deep, because happily, on the film, you can't see that Max didn't take him deep enough and Ron went all the way only because his straight-arm drove that defensive man into the ground almost up to his knees.

"Vince," the producer says, "remember that you can get your cue for that from this camera over here."

If I get my cue from that camera over there I'll probably still trip over that cord. If I remember the cord I probably won't remember to get my cue from that camera over there.

"Now here's Paul Hornung," I say, walking back to my seat and holding the mike cord away from me like it's a snake. "He has some tips on kicking extra points."

"Vince?" a disembodied voice from somewhere up above says, and I have no idea where it's coming from.

"Yes?"

"When you say that," the disembodied voice says, "you can look at camera 3."

"Look at what?" I say, because camera 3 means as much to me as Draw-4 or R-Turn-In-L-Zig-Out would mean to this disembodied voice.

"That camera to your right," the disembodied voice says.

"It's just like a Wednesday practice," Red Cochran says. "Chaos. A debacle."

"It'll be fine," the producer says.

So at eight o'clock we go on and I don't know whether it's fine or not but when it's over everyone says it was fine and we shake hands all around. Don Hutson goes back to Racine and Red Cochran and I go back to the office.

8:40 P.M.

Phil Bengtson and Norb Hecker are in the outer office grading the defensive line and the defensive backs off the film of the Bears game. Bill Austin and Tom Fears are in the back room waiting for Red and me, and we get down to work on our goal-line offense.

Anything you do inside the opponent's 10-yard line is designed to go all the way or to set up something that will. You have to remember that the end zone is only 10 yards deep, though, which does not give you a lot of room, and so it's a traffic jam and your goal-line plays are basically quick-hitting power plays.

"We're pretty certain we're going to get a 6-1," I say, because in the last four years they've used that defense every time in this situation. "I think when we're in the Red we have an idea that the middle linebacker will move to a position opposite our fullback, but I haven't seen him do it. From the Blue you've got 64, 67 and 37, and that's enough, but on 37 we have to take the left linebacker with the tight end. Then I don't know how they can stop 36. All you need is a piece of these guys."

Our 36 is our fullback slant with Taylor carrying. To make it go all our left tackle and left guard have to do is drive out, taking the defensive end and tackle in the direction they want to go, and let Taylor run to daylight.

"They don't stop it," Bill Austin says. "We always get a couple of yards, at least."

We watch on the screen, once more, that futile, pathetic

goal-line offense of ours in our losing game with the other people a year ago. We have a first down on the 3-yard line and Paul Hornung loses 3 yards.

"This 78 or 79 is still good against them," I say. "Hornung was too slow, and Max should have blown back on this."

"This is where we get excited," Bill says, "and run a couple of plays in a hurry."

Taylor goes to the 1-foot line on our 34-Cross but can't quite make it. Then Bart Starr tries a quarterback sneak and loses 2 yards and, since last year, I've seen enough of this.

"All right. Let's put up the defenses," I say to Red Cochran, and he goes to the blackboard. "The 6-1 first. From the Brown Right you've got 45, 29-Pitchout, 28, 36 and 34-X. You've got 64 from the Blue but do you think we can shoot a 67 and a 37 at them?"

"The 37 from the Blue?" Bill says. "Yes."

"Now let's take a 6-2," I say. "You've got your quick traps—20-T, 41-T, 61, 65, your weak-side 28-Sweep, 36, 34-X and 64 from the Blue, and 22. Against the 4-4 you have 24, 41-Trap, 45, 29-Pitchout, 22 and 20-T, but I think we have to go for the Do-Dad every time."

The Do-Dad is a type of cooperative blocking employed when a linebacker lines up behind a lineman and they start to deal—one of them going to the left and the other to the right. One of the blockers drives to the outside point of the first defender and the other man drives to the inside of the same defender. If that defender moves to the inside, the man who drives to the outside lets him go and takes the man behind him, and vice versa.

"Now we've got their Frisco," I say, "and then their 4-3."

"This is the way they handled the flare against the Forty-Niners on the goal line," Tom Fears says, handing me a sheet of the yellow lined paper with his diagram of how the other people defended the flare—the wide pass route to the flat by a back—when San Francisco tried it against them two weeks ago.

"Here it is in the movies," Bill Austin says as he starts the projector.

"Both the middle linebacker and the right linebacker move with the fullback flare," I say. I reason that, as I have always thought, their middle linebacker is keying on our fullback. Therefore, if we flare our fullback and run our halfback on a quick trap, we may be able to move that middle linebacker out of there without having to block him. And that would be a blessing, although you still have to block those two big tackles.

"Okay gentlemen," I say, standing up. "That's enough. We've either solved it or we haven't. What time is it?"

"A quarter to ten," Red Cochran says.

9:55 P.M.

I'm having my third hamburger of the day at Proski's. Andy Uram, who was a great back under Bernie Bierman at Minnesota and, in the late thirties and early forties for the Packers, is here, and Tim Cohane and a couple of others are having a discussion about whether there is any opportunity left today in football for coaching creativeness.

"Excuse me," someone says, tapping me on the shoulder and then handing me a pen and a piece of paper. "I have a thirteen-year-old son who thinks you and all the Packers are terrific. Would you mind giving me your autograph? His name is Bob."

I think this one really has a son. Half the time I suspect that, for reasons that are unfathomable to me, they want these autographs for themselves.

"Thanks a lot," he says. "Are you going to win on Sunday?"

He seems like a nice guy, but they ask that so often. What do they think the answer will be? Will I say that no, I don't think we'll win, that we'll probably get our blocks knocked off and lose by 40 points?

"We hope to win," I say.

"Well, good luck," he says.

In the discussion someone is saying that football coaching is a science and not an art. They have been playing this game, he says, since 1869 and, under the rules, there are only so many things, or combinations of things, you can do on the offense or defense with eleven men. In almost a century these have just about all been tried, and even when a coach comes up with a variation that seems to be inspirational it is really based on his knowledge of what has been done before and what can and can't be done by combining the talents of eleven men. Therefore it is scientific and not artistic.

"But at the same time," Cohane is saying, "it can't be an exact science because the players the coach moves around

82

on his blackboard and then on the field are not inanimate, obedient objects like chess pieces. They're unpredictable human beings. Right?"

He has turned to me. I agree, but I am too tired to get into this.

"All I know," I say, "is that this has become a game for madmen."

"Right," Cohane says.

He once proposed that the perfect name for the perfect coach would be Simple Simon Legree.

11:05 P.M.

The rain has stopped by the time I get home. Even if it doesn't start again before practice tomorrow those fields will still be so soggy that our offensive backs, receivers and defensive backs won't be able to make their moves with authority. But then it'll be wet for the other people, too.

I find the *Milwaukee Journal*, but I can't find the *Green Bay Press Gazette*. I turn to the sports pages. Oliver Kuechle doesn't have a column today but Chuck Johnson has been talking to our opponent's coach.

"The Packers are so well-rounded, offensively and defensively," the other coach says, "that they're a hard team to play. You get no breather no matter who's on the field."

He is conceding nothing in balance, though, it says, because his own club has always been tough on defense and now his offense has scored 119 points in winning their first three games. He agrees with what Wally Cruice told us, that their pass protection has improved to go with their new quarterback, but I remember what Phil Bengtson said. After watching the film of their offense against the Colts he said that Marchetti was giving that tackle fits all afternoon. On the other hand, on any given afternoon Marchetti might give anybody fits.

What it will all come down to again on Sunday, I'm thinking, is that we will both try to do what we do best. We know everything they can do and they know everything we can do, so we will both go with our strength. That is, basically, what it must come down to week after week if you are going to continue to win in this league.

Change is good, of course. The element of surprise may have temporary value, which is why we are putting in some of that Double-Wing for Sunday, but both of us can be reasonably sure that the other team is not really going to change because only a grossly inferior team should ever depart or deviate from its strength to win. Even surprise should be based on deception and rapidity of maneuver and not radical change, but I have known coaches who, giving their opponents too much credit, went for the radical change. I have seen them change their basic offenses and defenses for one big game and, although this may work occasionally, it is still fundamentally false because a team expresses a coach's personality and its own personality, and this doesn't change from week to week.

"In football," I was saying to Vincent once, "as in anything else, if you alter your personality just to accomplish something you're not being true. You're being dishonest. But I've seen coaches who, seeing that someone had success with something, immediately tried to take it for themselves. It didn't work because it didn't fit them. It didn't express their personalities."

"Oh, I don't know," Vincent said. "You've used what you learned from others."

"That's right," I said. "You have to start somewhere. When you start to coach you coach the system you played, but you begin almost immediately to discard what doesn't fit you or your material, and you look for what does."

"I don't see what's wrong with that," Vincent said.

"There's nothing wrong with it, up to a point," I said. "All of us are takers, but if a person can't add something to what he takes from others he should get out. Unfortunately some people will always be takers, and if they don't get out they don't get very far. In all my years of coaching I have never been successful using somebody else's play."

We have that robbery film. Our coaches made up a film of the successful plays of the other coaches in this league. The Forty-Niners run the best screen play in the business, and I can still see Hugh McElhenny hurting us with it my first year here. We took off seven or eight of those Forty-Niner screens. The Browns run the pitchout better than the rest of us, and we've got that, but none of them really work for us.

The reason they don't work for us is the reason our sweep doesn't work with our success for them. You have a special way of coaching your number one play that can't be picked off the films, and even when the coaches change—and the

Forty-Niners went from Buck Shaw to Frankie Albert and then Red Hickey—the carry-over player personnel makes it go. They make it go because they know it's their top-priority play and they have a confidence in it that it is impossible to give them in a play they know you have stolen.

When you come to think of it, this is really a tribute to the basic integrity of football.

THURSDAY

7:50 A.M.

Marie is sleeping soundly, so she must be feeling better. When Susan and I leave the house the weather has improved, if only slightly. It is not raining or misting, but with this fog the fields won't have a chance to dry.

"Don't forget me," Susan says.

I was just thinking that, in addition to those goal-line plays we've already put in, we should also be able to run away from that 56 when he moves over in front of our full-back if we use either a weak-side off-tackle play or our weak-side sweep. That means, though, that I've got to get Lew Carpenter in there for Max McGee, because he's a stronger blocker, and I can only do that once before they spot it.

I drop Susan at her school and miss the light when some-body else, in the front car in line, must be thinking about his own goal-line plays. When I come out of St. Willebrord's the fog has started to lift.

8:35 A.M.

"Statistics are nice to look at," Bud Lea has quoted Phil Bengtson as saying, "but winning is the only important thing."

I am having breakfast at Sneezer's and Max McGee and Jesse Whittenton are at the next counter. In his story Bud points out that the league statistics show we have allowed the fewest points, fewest first downs, fewest total yards and fewest yards passing, while we have the most interceptions and most yards returned with intercepted passes.

I am pretty well satisfied with that for a defensive record, and one of the reasons for it is right here having breakfast at that next counter—Mr. Jesse Whittenton. He is out of Texas Western and now a Green Bay restaurateur, and he is as close to being a perfect defensive back as anyone in the league. Speed offensively is great but speed in your defensive backs is a must and Jesse has that. He can run with any halfback or receiver in the league and, like Hank Gremminger, he is a great student of opponents. He has studied everything about all of them, including the expressions on their faces that, when they come up to the line, may tell him something about what they are going to run. He has such a complete book on all the veterans, in fact, that he says he would much rather go against the best receiver in the league than a first-year man he is looking at for the first time.

"The trouble with this job," he once said, "is that it's all out in the open where everyone can see it. You make one mistake and they complete a pass for a TD and millions watch you running behind the other guy, looking like a fool."

He is not a worrier, though, while Hank, the other great student, says he never sleeps well before a game. When we're playing Baltimore, Gremminger says he sees Lenny Moore running his patterns all night long, but then Moore can catch a 2-yard hitch and run it 90 yards and his slant-in-and-up and his square-out are enough to keep anyone awake nights.

Jesse says he has his hardest time against the Eagles, covering Pete Retzlaff, who doesn't have great speed but always comes off the line at the same pace and then breaks off quickly in Kyle Rote style. On the other hand, Jesse and Del Shofner of the Giants roomed together when they were both defensive backs with the Rams, and the way Jesse covers him now, he must have made a book on how Shofner does everything from brushing his teeth to putting on his socks.

When you consider how few mistakes Jesse makes out there you would mark him as a conservative, but the fact is that he's impulsive and a gambler. I remember that 1961 regular season game with the Giants in Milwaukee. If we won we would sew up the Western Division title but they were leading us 17-13 early in the fourth quarter. They had the ball on their own 8 and Alex Webster broke off tackle and was at the 30 when Jesse came across and got into it. Instead of going for the tackle he went for the steal, and he got the ball, and four plays later Jimmy Taylor busted into the end zone and we won it and the title 20-17.

It was a gamble, because if Jesse missed that ball Webster would have been at least to midfield before Willie Wood or Johnny Symank could have caught him. The successful gambler always has his reasons, though, and Jesse says he reasoned that Webster already had his first down and at that stage of the game a long drive could have ruined us. The Giants are good at killing the clock, and Jesse said later he had already made up his mind that if they threw a pass to his side he was going for the ball.

"Then when they ran and I saw Alex holding that ball out and high," he said, "it looked like a good risk."

After the season was over Jesse and Webster were in the annual players' golf tournament in Miami, and they missed their plane connection for the Pro Bowl Game. When they arrived late for practice they were fined $50 apiece.

"You should pay it for both of us," Webster said to Jesse. "All that publicity you got stealing the ball from me is what got you into this game."

It's a frustrating job, though, that these defensive backs have, and I've seen many of them cry. I've seen big, tough defensive linemen cry, too, but defensive backs more than the others because theirs is a real burden, no matter how hard you try to make their jobs easier, to lessen that burden just a little.

You cannot play defensive halfback or safety without knowing where your help is at all times and so you must know not only your own job but also the other three, and the assignments on each play of the three linebackers as well. We have our basic defenses—our 4-3, 4-4, Frisco, 6-1 and Gap, with the four defensive linemen and three linebackers positioned in the gaps between the offensive linemen. We can call any one of eleven defenses, however, and then have our variations off them. The assignments are often the same, of course, but a man must still recognize what his assignment is and what everybody else does in each defense and its variations.

So we give them, say, that halfback key. On that first step that the offensive halfback takes they can spot whether it is a run or a pass, but they have to spot it at the same time as they are starting their coverage of their receivers and analyzing their actions. In this league, though, there is also a time factor that they must learn to use. On a pass a quarterback has, on the average, 3.5 seconds to unload that ball, and the good defensive backs, like the good jockeys, should have clocks in their heads. By experience they should know when three seconds are up and, if that quarterback still hasn't unloaded, they should start to drift in the direction in which he is now looking. That is why good defensive backs are so hard to come by and why, when you get a new one who looks like he may make it, you are so reluctant to let him go.

You draft most of them, as we did Adderley, as offensive backs and when they can't make it there we turn them over to Norb Hecker. If they played defense in college it was probably some sort of comparatively simple zone, but the problem is physical as well as mental. As their training and experience have been mainly on the offense they are accustomed, when taking a pass, to grab it and continue to go in the direction of that pass. On the defense, when they make that grab, they must go against the grain, against the direction of that throw, and at first even the most agile of them are all crossed legs and wooden hands.

"Now that I've finally got his legs straightened out," Norb will say of one of them, after weeks in training camp of throwing to them short, long, to one side and then the other, "his hands are going bad, but who knows?"

It's hard to know. A new kid, who has never seen a receiver with moves like Max McGee, is trying to cover Max, and another is trying to stay with Boyd Dowler. At the same time they're trying to remember everything Norb has been pumping into their heads at his meetings. You have a tendency, of course, to compare them right on that same field with your veterans. But you have to remember that the big thing the veterans have going for them is the experience they've had working as a unit, and the problem is to project what promise the new ones show into what they may be in the future.

"Consider these factors," I'm reading now in Bud Lea's story as he quotes our opponent's publicity man. "Our new-found offensive punch, responsible for 119 points in three games, will meet a defensive unit that has allowed three opponents only 7 points. The Packers' bulldozing ground game will be challenged by our defense that has begrudgingly given up only 203 yards on the ground.

"Our league-leading passer, with a 64.6 completion average

good for 783 yards, meets the Packer defensive backfield that has allowed opponents only 46.1 completions and has already intercepted twelve passes. The game pits perhaps the finest offensive line against what many consider the league's top defensive line. The prize is uncontested first place in the Western Conference race and a whole week to enjoy it."

He talks like a publicity man—"new-found offensive punch" . . . "bulldozing ground game" . . . "begrudgingly given" . . . "the game pits" . . . "the prize is uncontested first place." But he's right when he says that it shapes up as quite a ball game. In fact, it may be the ball game of the year.

"We've had things pretty much our own way so far," Phil Bengston is saying in the story. "This should be a real good test for us. We're anxious to meet them."

I agree, and I meant it when I told them yesterday that I was looking forward to this. We plot and prepare all winter and spring and then we work them hard from the middle of July and all of it has but one purpose. We want to perfect ourselves so that we can win with less struggle and increasing ease, but the strange thing is that it's not the easy wins we ostensibly seek but rather the difficult struggles to which we really look forward.

8:55 A.M.

When I turn onto Oneida Avenue the deserted practice fields to the left are like a lush, damp pasture under the low, gray skies, and the gray, canvas-padded seven-man and two-man blocking sleds, standing there alone, look like lonely forgotten cattle.

The boys are here early, though. There are more than a dozen cars already parked outside the dressing rooms—a good sign on a Thursday that they are starting to come up for a game—and among them is Dave Hanner's green and white pickup truck.

Dave Hanner's real name is Joel but his nickname is Dave and they call him Hawg. He is our left defensive tackle. He was born in Arkansas and lives there in West Memphis, where he is a soil conservationist in the off-season. The Packers drafted him out of Arkansas University eleven years ago. He is thirty-two now and it is going to be a sad day in Green Bay when the years get him because he has not only been All-Pro five times but there is nobody on this squad who is better-liked than big, easygoing, quiet Dave with that chaw of tobacco in his right cheek and his constant weight problem.

"What do you weigh?" I say to him each year when he arrives in camp in his truck.

"Oh, I'll be all right," big, blond Dave says, with that slow smile.

"So what do you weigh?" I say, slapping his stomach. "You look like you've got a lot of it here."

"Oh," he says, with that smile again, "about 270."

"That's too much," I say.

"I was 266 coming in last year," he says. "I'll get it off."

"You'll have to," I say.

I know he'll get it off. I know he'll be down to 260 again when we're ready to go, but it is more of a struggle for him each year, and it is something to watch.

He grew up, Dave did, as a farmboy and he still keeps farm hours and I guess he always will. Breakfast in camp is at seven-thirty, but Dave is up at six-thirty and you know he will always be in bed by ten. He is in and out of that dining room before anyone else, because he watches his diet, and on the practice field, wearing that old, dark blue baseball cap to protect that fair head and forehead from the hot sun, he really sweats. I remember, too, when one Wednesday in 1961 he had his appendix out and he played eleven days later.

"When I was drafted by the Packers," Jim Ringo said once, "I had to go get an atlas to find out where Green Bay is."

"That's nothin'." Dave said. "I didn't know where it was either, but I came up with another boy and we took a plane from Chicago. The plane stopped and we heard the stewardess say something about Green Bay so we got off. After the plane left we found out she was sayin', 'Oshkosh. Next stop Green Bay.' So we had to take a train up from there."

Dave says that those first few years he played with the Packers his neighbors back in Arkansas had never heard of Green Bay or the National Football League. Now that the Packers have won a title and the game was nationally televised, he says, they finally know what he does when he leaves home in July for five months every year.

In those twice-a-day meetings in training camp Dave is now like the college senior repeating a course. In that biology lab, if he hasn't found a paper cup or an empty tape container, he sits off to one side, near an open window, so he can unload his tobacco juice, and he clips his nails or looks out the window. When we get into the new material, though, he is as avid a student as any of them because he knows he never had much speed and has less now and he must concentrate to compensate. He will ask more questions of Phil Bengston than the greenest first-year man, and when we put in a move that's unique for a game Dave can't wait to try it.

"Can I make that move today?" he'll ask Phil.

Dave has played in this league against so many ballplayers for so long that you might say he knows what they are going to do before they do it. Like Hank Jordan he is a great student of tip-offs, looking for how much weight the other guard has on that hand, whether his knuckles are white or not, that may tell whether he is going to drive block or pass block, and watching for that altered stance that is the sign he is going to pull out.

"It usually takes even a good guard two or three years to cover tip-offs," Dave says; "and when a tackle sees a guard tip, a center can't hardly come over and take him."

Jerry Kramer is always using Dave to perfect his own techniques, and they work together a lot in practice. Jerry will keep asking Dave to tell him any time he is tipping, and we all have the same respect for him. In the off-season, if we're looking to pick up an offensive lineman in a possible trade, we'll get that lineman's card out of the file and look at him in our movies and have our coaches' discussion on him. Then I'll call Dave down in West Memphis.

"What's your opinion of him?" I'll say.

"Well, he's got good speed," Dave may say, "and he pulls well and trap blocks all right but he's not strong straight ahead."

With that chaw in his cheek and in those rumpled slacks and sports shirt, Dave will never be mistaken for Max McGee or Paul Hornung. When he is out on the field, though, in that gold helmet and Packer jersey and gold pants he looks like the rest of them, and he is just as sophisticated as Max and as worldly-wise as Paul about this game, and he is just as good at the position he plays.

"Morning, coach," he says to me now. He is getting out of his slacks and sports shirt in front of his dressing stall.

"How are you, Joel?" I say. "Did you tell me you need a single for Sunday?"

"Yes, sir, I do," he says. "I'd appreciate that."

I gave him the ticket and he gives me $6 because any tickets they get in addition to the one we give them for each game they must pay for. It is something that their friends and the free-loaders who zero in on professional athletics do not understand.

Gone now from this dressing room is that lazy, laconic, leisurely atmosphere of Tuesday and that freer, gayer air of Wednesday. They are preoccupied now, getting out of their street clothes and into their sweatclothes. You can feel the tension starting to grow, and I must keep them loose. Particularly, I must keep that offensive team loose, because they are the ones who tighten up, and they have got to go out there and block and run and pass with abandon if they are going to move that ball on Sunday.

With the defensive linemen and linebackers you do not have that problem because defensive football is a game of abandon anyway, and they have to be hell-for-leather types to play it at all. Tackling is easier to teach and keep tuned than blocking simply because it is more natural. If a man is running down the street with everything you own, you won't let him get away. That's tackling.

I sit down in the office and look over Red Cochran's file of goal-line plays. I am satisfied with most of them. I have my doubts about our 41-Trap, which is a trap on the defensive left tackle.

"I wonder about this 41-Trap," I say to Bill and Red, and thinking of that big number 76 who will be just off Jim Ringo's left shoulder when our opponents are in their goal-line defense. "This guy Ringo has to take is a big, strong man, and if Jim can't hold him this hole will close and we don't have much room there as is."

"But Ringo doesn't have to drive him," Bill says. "He cuts him down anyway."

When the Packers drafted Jim out of Syracuse in 1953 he weighed only 205 pounds. In those days the defenses were playing five-man lines, with a big middle guard over the center, and Les Bingaman of Detroit weighed 320 pounds.

"Do you think I should try pro ball?" Jim asked Ben Schwartzwalder, who coached him at Syracuse.

"Do you think you can make it?" Ben said.

"I don't know," Jim said.

"You'll never know," Schwartzwalder said, "until you try it. If you don't try it you'll always have that doubt."

The Packers were training in Grand Rapids, Minnesota,

92

that year. Jim weighed 210 pounds when he reported, and after about ten days he and a guard from Wisconsin took off together.

"I was getting the hell kicked out of me," Jim says, "and I was homesick. Do you know what that means? It's the most awful feeling."

Jim says he had 90¢ in his pocket, but the guard's father had a summer place in Rhinelander, Wisconsin, and some friends picked the two of them up in camp. Then the guard loaned Jim $70 to get back home to Easton, Pennsylvania, where Jack Vainisi, the Packers' business manager and chief talent scout who worked so hard to build the Packers and then died so suddenly just before we won the Western Division title in 1960, and Chuck Drulis, the line coach, reached him by phone.

"My wife was the one who made me come back," he says. "She asked me if I wanted to think of myself for the rest of my life as a quitter, so I came back. Then, when you're still getting your block knocked off, you start finding ways to compensate for it."

One of the factors that helped to make Jim Ringo was the elimination of those odd-man defensive lines with that big middle guard on the center's head, and we did it with our offensive line splits. In the odd-man line the tackles positioned on the outside shoulder of the offensive guards. When we shifted the guard an extra foot it widened the gap between the defensive tackle and the middle guard over center. If the defensive tackle stayed in, the offensive tackle moved out, widening another gap, so the effect was to put that defensive tackle in a position where he couldn't be right.

This forced them into the 4-3 defense. The tackles simply had to stay inside and play on the head, and not the outside shoulder, of the offensive guards. The defensive ends were forced to come inside to play the role of defensive tackles, with the corner linebackers to protect them outside, and the middle guard had to drop off the line and become a middle linebacker protecting against passes as well as runs.

This changed the whole game for the ends, who now, becoming tackles in play, needed size and strength plus the mobility they had needed previously, and also for the middle guard. Now he had to be much more mobile, for he was a free-lancer. It gave him the opportunity, because he is out there in the open where he can be seen, to take those glamour shots at the ball-carrier after the line strips the runner of blockers, and it made Sunday heroes of Joe Schmidt, Ray Nitschke, Sam Huff, Bill George and the rest.

It changed the game for the offensive center, too, because now the emphasis has to be on his agility and not his size. Instead of being required to move a monster playing him head-on he blocks to either side. These on-side blocks—on the side to which the play is going—are not usually the type requiring him to move the man. They're the cut-off type, where the blocker just injects himself between the defensive man and the play, but they require such agility on the part of a center that only a few others in the league besides Ringo —John Morrow of the Browns—Bob DeMarco of the Cardinals and that new boy with the Vikings, Mickey Tinglehoff— can make them consistently with effectiveness.

Jim is not only quick but he stays on you. A few years ago a Redskin coach said he had been watching movies of their opponents against the Packers. He said that in five games he never saw Ringo miss an assignment, and when we graded our players after our game with Cleveland in 1961 Jim got the highest marks ever handed out to a Packer. Just minutes before that game he had been lying on the rubbing table, getting injections to freeze fourteen boils, and it was so painful that tears had come to his eyes.

He will rise in anger with himself and his own team, and he becomes morose after a loss, but he has a lot of poise and leadership ability on that field. After looking over the defense, and as offensive captain, he often calls the blocks for the guards and tackles and, of course, he starts every play. He centers the ball between 850 and 900 times a season and more than a hundred times it is on the long pass-back for punts, points after touchdowns and field goals. That snap must be done with split-second timing, and I remember the hours we spent arguing about that quarterback exchange in the coaches' office at West Point.

One of us would be the quarterback and another the center and a third had a ruler and a piece of chalk. He'd stand the ruler upright on a desk and hold the chalk at a certain height. When the quarterback said "Hut!" the center would snap the ball and the third man would drop the chalk. If the chalk hit the desk before the slap of the ball into the quarterback's hands he'd raise the chalk slightly on the next try. We were trying to determine the difference between the time required to snap the ball back with the full wrist turn, as they were

94

doing at the Point, as against the quarter-turn I was recom-
mending. I felt that the ball would be presented in a better
position to be handled for passing and handing off. Later,
to replace the ruler and chalk, we borrowed a device with a
marble in it from the physics lab.

As it turned out, the quarter-turn was faster than the full
wrist turn. It was only a fraction of a second, but that is
what we deal with in this game. On the snap signal the
center starts his pass motion, every lineman starts his motion
and every back starts his motion, except for the quarterback,
who must wait until he gets the ball. Obviously, any sub-
stantial time-loss there will defeat you, so even that fraction
will make a difference.

Those first few years here in Green Bay were tough for
Ringo, not only on the field but off. The Packers were tail-
ing the league in those days, and one afternoon Jim's
daughter Michelle came home from school crying and said,
"Daddy, are you a bum?" When her classmates kept insisting
that all the Packers were bums, the Ringos took her out of
school, and when the anonymous phone-callers became abu-
sive they had their phone removed.

"You can't really know what it means to win," Jim says,
"unless you've lost."

Now I go to the blackboard and diagram for Phil and
Norb the opposition's defenses that I want them to set up
against us in practice.

"And give us a lot of blitzes," I say. "You should be in
the two 4-3's and the Frisco, the 4-3 Zone and the 4-3
Combo. Also give us the 4-3 Man-to-Man."

"You want the 4-3 Man-to-Man?" Phil says.

"Yes, and any time they're in it they're blitzing. So you've
got your 4-3's, your Frisco, 4-4 and 6-2."

"What about the 6-1?" Phil says.

"Yes. This is a good time to practice your Storm, and I'll
tell you what I'll do. I'll call short-yardage situations out
there today and you go into your Storm."

When our opponent is in that 6-1, I'm thinking, with
those big brutes storming we're not going to be able to hold
them all on that line of scrimmage. Somebody is going to
penetrate.

"And Bill," I say, "against that 6-1 you've got to tell your
guards to pull deep. There's no reason why not. We're all
right then even if they get some penetration."

That's enough of that, and we are ready for our meetings. When I turn from the board big Ron Kramer is filling a cup at our coffeemaker just inside the door.

"Oh, excuse me, coach," he says, dropping his head. "I'm sorry."

"That's all right," I say, and I follow him into the dressing room. "Okay everybody, let's go. We had a good workout yesterday and we'll put on pads today. We'll have short meetings first, though. I want the quarterbacks in with me."

Bart Starr and Johnny Roach follow me back into the coaches' room. As I close the door I can hear Bill Austin starting with the rest of the offensive team.

"Now we want to go over our pass blocking," he says.

Starr and Roach sit down at the table and open their notebooks. I sit down across from them, and I have the listing of the plays we have been deciding on since Monday, and now I will give them our game plan.

Because of the enormous load he must carry in the way we play the game in this league, you spend more time with your quarterback and his back-up man than you do with any of the others. Without a good quarterback you just don't operate. And so every year every club is looking for some promising college senior, not to replace their present quarterback, because few can make it that first year, but for the future.

Since in the T formation he handles the ball on every play, and because so much of the pro attack has to do with passing, a quarterback must have sure hands and be an excellent passer. His I.Q. must be above average, because he must not only be able to absorb the coach's game plan each week but he must also have a thorough knowledge of what everyone does on every play, and he must know the opponent, the qualities and characteristics of each individual on the other team.

He should be strong physically and able to take punishment when those 270-pounders unload on him, and he should have enough height to see his receivers over those opposing linemen. Eddie LeBaron, at Washington and Dallas, would have been an all-time great if he had been tall. He has a fine mind and he has been a great ball-handler, passer and competitor, but at 5-7 he has had trouble staying in that pocket and seeing out of it, and he has had to resort to those roll-out passes and play-type passes off the fake run.

A quarterback must have great poise, too, and he must

The game is the big show but it's the practice sessions that mean the difference between a peak and a poor performance. Here Lombardi, a relentless perfectionist, directs his players during a training drill. (VERNON J. BIEVER PHOTO)

The payoff. Packer fullback Chuck Mercein (30) runs to daylight and a third period touchdown in the 1968 NFL Western Conference playoff game against the Los Angeles Rams. Green Bay won 28-7. (VERNON J. BIEVER PHOTO)

It was 13 below zero in Green Bay during the 1967 NFL championship contest between the Packers and the Dallas Cowboys but the action was searing hot. Flaps down, Skipper Lombardi anxiously observes the action from the sidelines. (VERNON J. BIEVER PHOTO)

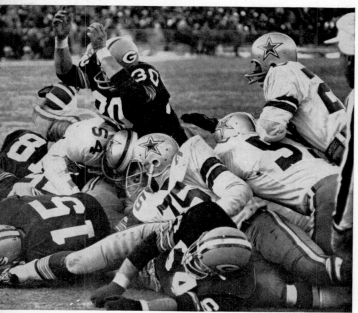

The touchdown that won a title. As Chuck Mercein (30) throws up his hands joyfully, the Packers' great quarterback, Bart Starr (15), plunges over the goal line for the heart-stopping, last seconds touchdown that beat Dallas. Final score: 21-17. (VERNON J. BIEVER PHOTO)

Frenzy in Green Bay. Freezing but delirious Packer fans rip down the metal goal posts after the victory over Dallas. (VERNON J. BIEVER PHOTO)

The famous Packer sweep play in action against the Oakland Raiders in the Super Bowl contest at Miami, January 14, 1968. With offensive guards Gale Gillingham (68) and Jerry Kramer (64) moving to protect the runner, quarterback Starr (15) hands the ball off to halfback Donny Anderson (44). (VERNON J. BIEVER PHOTO)

The kind of offense that ripped the Raider line to shreds. Packer fullback Ben Wilson (36), the game's leading ground gainer, tear through the Oakland defense for a hefty hunk of yardage. Victor went to Green Bay by the one-sided margin of 33-14. (VERNON BIEVER PHOTO)

Sweet moment of success. The leader of the 1968 Super Bow champs is carried off the field in triumph by his exultant players It was the second straight Super Bowl win for the peerless Packe coach and the third record-breaking year in a row that his super charged athletes had won the NFL championship. (VERNON J. BIEVER PHOTO)

not be panicked by what the defense does or his own offense fails to do. He must know the characteristic fakes and patterns of his ends and backs and anticipate the break before the receiver makes it. Then there are those times when, by the nature of its rush, the defense overextends and leaves itself open to a run, so the quarterback who can also run has a great advantage.

If you find all this in one man you have found a special person, and each year you try. Although you have more knowledge about the college quarterback than about anyone else you draft, the first-year quarterback, because of the complex intricacies of playing the position, is still the biggest question mark.

The great difference between the college game and the pro game is that they don't emphasize the pass as we do. They do not have the time to put in a complete passing attack, and the combination of passer and receivers is seldom found on one college squad. A college team may have a superior passer or a superior receiver, but every pro team has a superior passer and a number of superior receivers.

"I've been coaching for twenty-five years," the head coach of a Midwest school once told me, "and in all that time I've had just two superior passers. I've had a number of superior receivers, but when I've had the passer I've never had the receivers to go with him and vice versa."

At West Point I was a part of fine college football but at that first training camp with the pros, with the Giants at Salem, Oregon, in the summer of 1954, I was amazed. I was not surprised by what they did, because I had been studying it all in movies for six months, but the ease with which they accomplished it amazed me. I can still see the fluid motion Frank Gifford had while running the ball, the great hands Kyle Rote exhibited in catching it and the anticipation Charley Conerly had in releasing the ball.

Everything we taught those backs was grasped by them immediately, and Conerly possessed exceptional poise. He was a master at getting rid of the ball under pressure, and when his receivers were covered he had that rare knack of throwing it just a little off-target so that it could neither be intercepted nor called intentional grounding. The fans, who didn't know what Charley was doing, used to boo him unmercifully, but he threw for few interceptions and he seldom had to eat the ball. I've never coached a football player who had more courage.

Bill Swiacki, who had been a fine receiver at Columbia and with the Giants, was coaching the offensive ends and he was the first to give me a real understanding of the passing game—the pass routes, the faking and how they were coached. In college your receivers basically either hooked or went down on a fly route, and 80 percent of your time was spent on the running game and only 20 percent on passing. In the pros it was 50-50, with some teams spending even more time on their passing. Swiacki wanted us to throw almost all the time. We had some violent arguments over that, but I respected him. I respected his intelligence, his experience as a receiver that told him how much he could logically expect of others, his knowledge of the defensive secondaries and his creativity. These qualities I have been lucky to find again in Tom Fears.

"So let's take the 4-3 first," I am saying to my quarterbacks now. "On your running plays against the 4-3 remember the middle linebacker will key on the fullback, so you know that plays like 50, 51, 52, 53, 64, 65, 72 and 73 are good football plays."

So each year we try to find a quarterback in college, but everyone else is trying to find one, too. We draft one and we go to camp, and on that first day of practice the first thing we have to find out is if he can really throw. We have the passing drill with the centers and quarterbacks, and with the receivers making their various cuts. Our new boy is back there with Starr and Roach, and everybody is looking because everybody knows this is important.

Starr throws and Roach throws and then our new boy takes his first snap from center. With all of us watching he steps back to where his pocket would be and he lets it go. Let's say he's impressive, because I remember one who was very impressive that first day. He could throw the long ball, he led his receivers well, his actions were fluid and he exuded the confidence a quarterback must have.

"We may have a natural here," I said to the other coaches on the way off the field. "This kid has the touch."

He had not had great coaching and he had some minor faults. He carried the ball so low that it took him too much time to get it up into passing position, and on his short passes he had a tendency to throw the ball down. We worked on these things in camp and we started to spot-play him in our pre-season games, and when he looked excellent we thought we had come up with a real find.

Then the bubble burst. When we tried him late in regular

league games he lost all his poise under pressure. He forgot the game plan he knew letter-perfect and couldn't find his receivers and he lost the quickness he had acquired in practice and he threw for interceptions. Of course, the team lost all confidence in him. He simply could not move the club. What leadership qualities he had seemed to possess were missing in action. I remember one veteran quarterback who lost them, too, when he began to believe that his receivers were dropping the ball on purpose as part of a plot to persecute him.

"Now I believe this right end is their weakest player," I'm telling Starr and Roach. "I don't mean he's a patsy, but he's not quite up to the rest of their talent. Therefore I believe we can sweep left. We can sweep right, too, of course, but also on the left their right corner back doesn't come up as fast on running plays as their left corner back does. Therefore 49-Weak should be a good play, too."

Starr and Roach make a note of this and look up and nod. Johnny Roach was a Single-Wing halfback at Southern Methodist but when they switched to the T they made him a quarterback. He was a third draft choice of the St. Louis Cardinals and in his first year they played him as a defensive back. In 1960 he was their quarterback, but before the next season started they traded him to the Cleveland Browns and we got him from them as a back-up man for Bart.

Some men are so obviously unhappy in utility roles that they show it. This hurts the morale of the team. When you put them in a game they don't perform up to their potential, but if Johnny Roach is unhappy in Starr's shadow you can't tell it from his attitude or his play. He has a good mind and an excellent memory, and if I need him I know that he has been hitting that playbook and that ready list just as hard as Bart.

Tom Moore, behind Paul Hornung, and Ken Iman, backing up Jim Ringo, are a couple of others and Lew Carpenter is a third. When we put Moore in against the Minnesota Vikings last year he picked up 159 yards rushing, and only Jimmy Taylor on this club has ever gained more in one game.

Lew Carpenter, whose younger brother Preston is with the Steelers, is in his ninth year, but no first-year man works harder from July into December than Lew. It is much easier for the younger ones you have on your bench, your first-year men and then your second-year men like Nelson Toburen and Ron Kostelnik. The first-year men are happy just to be aboard and the second-year men know they still have a lot to learn and that they still have the time. It is the older ones, like Lew Carpenter and Gary Knafelc and Johnny Symank, who still give you everything they've got and who have my deepest admiration. They keep you alive when you are hurt and in pain and would otherwise be dying in some game.

"Their left linebacker," I'm saying now, "has a tendency to play tight inside. He's very conscious of not letting the end release to his inside. Therefore, from the Brown, plays like 69 and 79 with zone blocking should be good out there."

In the Brown formation the fullback lines up behind the quarterback, rather than behind the right guard as in the Red. In zone blocking each offensive man takes the defensive man playing over him, and our 69 and 79, with that blocking, are plays that should be good against that tight linebacker, because our tight end can hook, or block, him in.

"Remember," I tell them, "that last year we hurt them with 60 and 61, right at them up the middle. When they closed o us, Taylor veered off, so they should be good plays again Also 50 and 51 from the Brown should be good, and that's the rundown on what we should be doing against the 4-3.

"Now on your passes, Max has proved he can beat that right corner man, that 44. Against the other guy, that 81, you've heard me say, and you know, we should stay away from any type of turn-in. Right?"

"Yes, sir," Starr says, and Roach nods.

"I think the defense next in importance that you'll see will be their 6-1. They seem to like to play it against us and it's usually their short-yardage defense. When you anticipate the 6-1, your 36 and 34-Cross, your 45 and 67 are the plays you should use. That's for short yardage, and the 45 is from the Red. Now what are your others besides those four? You have your 29-Pitchout to either side, and your other plays are your 38-Toss and your 69.

"The defense next in importance is the Frisco. Your better plays here are 43 and 22 either way. Now what else? Your 65 is good, as you know, and your 36 and 34, into the Frisco hole. Then you've also got your 28, 38-T and 39-T.

"They also play a 6-2, but I don't think you'll see much of it. The characteristics of their 6-2 is that their ends are up the field. Go at that weak side with 36, 34-Cross and 22 and 64 from the Blue. There's nothing wrong with the 35-Cross, 43 and 65 to go at the strength, and remember to stay inside the ends with the exception of the 39-Toss.

100

"Now the 4-4. The way you recognize it is by the position of the tackles. The tackles are a little wider and slightly off the ball. Your best plays are the quick traps, sweeps and slants using do-dad blocking."

When I finish with the quarterbacks we exchange rooms with Bill Austin. He brings the offensive linemen into the coaches' office and Starr and Roach and I rejoin the other backs and receivers in the dressing room. I go to the blackboard and put up their Frisco Strong and diagram our Wham play with the key block by the halfback on the defensive tackle.

"Now let's go back a little over our passing game," I say. "We go into the Red and they go into a Combination, and your better plays are the turn-ins to the tight end and the flanker and your crossing patterns. From the Red you'll also meet a 6-1."

"Coach?" Paul Hornung says. "At what times does the middle linebacker go to the weak side when the fullback swings?"

"Only in the Zone," I say. "The only time he goes away from the fullback is when they've got a Zone on."

"I understand."

"Now they're playing a lot of pass defense," I say. "From the Blue we've got all individual patterns to the weak-side end. All your swing passes can be run from the Double-Wing, and also from the Double-Wing you've got the Detroit pass from the Red. Boyd?"

"Yes?" say Boyd Dowler, our flanker back.

"With your guy," I say, thinking of that left corner back, that 81 again, "on our 96 I'd fake it in and go. He can be beat deep."

"Yes, sir."

"He's a guesser and a gambler. He makes a lot of mistakes, and somebody gets behind him every game. You have to recognize, though, that he's a great athlete and they've quieted him down. There was a time when he was always playing his own game, and the safety man was trying to cover for him all the time, but that's not as predominantly true as it used to be."

Years ago, I'm thinking, we'd all see those mistakes he'd make and we'd all put in something to take advantage of them, and he'd intercept. One year he intercepted fourteen, which is still a record for a single season, and it was almost as if he had set a trap for all of us.

"Okay," I say. "Now we've got to be mentally ready to play this game. Believe me, nothing would please me more than to beat this club. They're great talkers and all they talk about is how they can beat the Packers. You've got to be mentally ready."

When a ball club flattens out it is because they go mentally and psychologically, rather than physically, stale. A well-conditioned athlete may be exhausted at the end of a game but, barring injury, he can come back with twenty-four hours' rest. He does not lose his vigor, he loses his urge. That is why we go to such pains to keep them from becoming bored by this week-after-week routine.

Everything we do, in these meetings or on the practice field, we do only for short periods. We never stay on one phase of this game for any great length of time, because if I get bored coaching the same thing over and over they are going to get bored learning it, although there are those times when they are not getting something and I must fight that urge to keep them at it until they do.

In this league, when you have two evenly matched teams and one wins by two or three touchdowns, the other was not mentally sharp. This was the plight of the Giants when we beat them 37-0 in that 1961 championship game, because three games earlier we had needed that Whittenton steal on Webster to beat them 20-17. They came into that title game after a season-long struggle and they never got the big play that might have snapped them out. I must believe that we were ready to beat anyone that day, but I remember an interception that popped out of Erich Barnes' hands and that potential TD pass that was just a little long and bounced off Kyle Rote's fingers.

When you are flat you're always looking for that big play or that big man who will bring you out of it. When I was with the Giants it was Frank Gifford who would reel off a run. Johnny Unitas has come up with the big throw consistently for Baltimore and Bobby Layne used to do it with Detroit and Pittsburgh. Ray Nitschke has a lot of this on the defense for us, and on the offense, when he's in shape, we get it from Hornung. If it isn't Paul, Jimmy Taylor will bust through and, when two or three hit him, bull them off and pick up our whole club at the same time.

Sometimes it will be the opponents who suddenly, and by something they do, pick your club up. One of their players will swing at one of yours, or they will pile on. On the sideline, because you have been trying everything you know but with no success, you have been praying for something like this, and now it's a different ball game.

For a Sunday game, mental sharpness has to start coming on Wednesday or, at the latest, by Thursday. We had that good practice yesterday and I could feel the beginnings of that tension when I walked in here two hours ago. We should be all right out there today.

"So let's go," I say now. "Let's get those pads on and get down there."

"How to go!" somebody says.

I start through the door to the coaches' room to get into my sweatclothes and rain jacket. Jerry Kramer is coming out and he has that small-boy half-grin on his face again. He has been at the coffeemaker and is smuggling a doughnut out between the pages of his playbook.

"Good morning, coach," he says.

11:10 A.M.

"Let's go now," I say. "Who leads today?"

They have been loosening up, the offense in white jerseys and the defense in green. It is starting to mist again and it may turn to rain any minute, so I want to get the grass drill out of the way and get down to business.

"The Thin Man!" someone shouts. "Give us The Thin Man."

Johnny Roach is 6-4, but he weighs only 200 pounds and, compared with the rest of them, he looks thin. He leads them, their feet slightly spread, bending over and touching first one foot and then the other.

"One-two-one," they are chanting with him like a male chorus. "One-two-two. One-two-three . . ."

"Come on!" I shout, "Pick it up! Pick it up!"

"Yeah, Roach," Quinlan shouts, two counts behind the others. "Let's pick it up!"

When they finish they run for the far goalposts and make the turn. As they start back I see that Hank Jordan is leading them.

"Jordan threw off the flu?" I say to Phil Bengston.

"Henry's a rugged boy," Phil says, "and he wants to be ready for this one."

"Look at all those green shirts loafing back there!" I holler at them as they run by. "Get up there, you green shirts!"

Bob Schulze and Al Sampson, the sports telecasters, and Art Daley, the sports editor of the *Green Bay Post Gazette*, are watching. We move to the seven-man blocking sled and Phil and Norb Hecker and I climb up on the back of it and the offensive line makes the first charge.

"No! No!" I holler, before the sled even comes to rest. "Together! Together! Not like a typewriter!"

It is that split-second timing, and they must all drive off the snap of the ball together and all hit as one. They know it, and they've all been doing it since July, and some of them have been doing it for eight or ten years, but you have to keep stressing and polishing that timing.

While the offensive line is re-forming, the defensive line makes its charge. They hit with good coordination and power, and the sled, with Phil and Norb and me weighting it, slides over the wet grass for at least 5 yards.

"Now the left shoulder," I say to the offensive line. "And let's pop"

"On three!" Starr says. "Set . . . 22 . . . 81 . . . Hut! . . . Hut! . . . Hut!"

It is that unrhythmic cadence. He varies the time interval between those "huts" so that no one can anticipate the snap of the ball, and it keeps our offensive line on-side, and the other people honest.

"Fuzzy!" I am hollering at Thurston. "For the love of Pete! You're walking and letting somebody else push it."

They have got to get that good explosion, driving off the front foot but keeping that spread base for the follow-up foot action, and when they get lazy they drop their tails and they have to cock first. They have to bring those tails up before they can drive, and that's where they lose that fraction of a second and that's all it takes to get beat.

"How to go!" I say the next time as we hear all those shoulder pads pop as one and feel that sled come up under us. "That's the way to go, Fuzz!"

When I played this game we were all position blockers. We took the first step to get into position and off the second step we launched our blocks. Today our whole running offense depends on the speed and power with which we drive off that line, and one of the refinements that contributes to the assurance and the quickness of those linemen is that rule blocking we used at West Point and that I carried over with me to the Giants.

Up to that time the Giants had been blocking according

to the defense they were facing on any play. Against a 5-1 a lineman would be responsible for a certain man, and against an Eagle defense he would be responsible for another. The defense dictated the man he was to block, so what this was, in effect, was a defensive approach to offensive football, and I will never forget that first meeting at Salem, Oregon, when I went to the board, knowing that they were skeptical of any "college stuff" I might want to introduce, and diagrammed and explained rule blocking.

"Center," I said, "drive the man over you. None, release and fan back."

A drive block is a shoulder block, and the center, knowing by the number of the play whether it was going to the right or left, would know which shoulder to use to keep his head between his opponent and the hole. If there was none—or no one—over him, he was to release—proceed ahead—deep enough to clear the line of scrimmage. Then he was to fan back, meaning block back into any pursuit that was coming. When we used this at the Point it was so effective and so vicious that our opponents, studying the film but able to pick up no pattern, tried to get it outlawed.

"Guard," I explained at that board, "cut off the man over you. None, release and seal the first inside linebacker."

A cut-off block is one used to prevent quick pursuit and in which you project yourself on all fours between the defensive man and the hole, getting your arm and shoulder beyond his inside leg. The man over you may be on your head, but in either gap, off your inside shoulder or outside shoulder, he is also considered to be over you. To "seal" simply means to seal a man off from the hole.

When I gave it to them, this rule blocking, for the first time at that board, it was completely foreign to them, and I could tell from the way they looked at one another and from their air of resignation that they thought I was crazy. They figured, Bill Austin told me later, that they would just have to break me into pro coaching. Jim Lee Howell was in his first year as head coach then, and he gave me full authority to put it in, and they came around to my way. That rule blocking simplified it for those linemen, because they no longer had to learn a different assignment for each defense. Now the defense was no longer calling the shots and they bought it big.

"All right! All right!" I holler. "Let's not stand around socializing. Let's go!"

Bill Austin has taken his offensive linemen off to one side, and on the sled Phil and Norb and I concentrate on the defensive linemen and linebackers. They make their initial charge, and then they pivot off the padded canvas and run diagonally, the first time to the right and the next time to the left. It is the principle of pursuit, rapid recovery from the initial charge and the block placed on you and movement toward the direction of the play when you see it is not coming toward you. Good pursuit is one of the distinguishing characteristics of a good defensive ball club.

"Come on! Come on!" I shout, because that Northeast wind has started up and I'm afraid this mist will turn to rain and we still have to work on that passing game. "Let's go! Let's go!"

Phil has his interior defensive linemen, his tackles and ends, pass rush against Austin's offensive linemen, who are pass blocking. Jimmy Taylor runs a circle route and draws the linebacker and Starr hits Ron Kramer on a slant-out in the open area.

"How to go, Jimmy!" I shout. I have to keep him a believer when he's not carrying the ball. "Real good move!"

Ron Kramer goes down from the closed-end position and hooks and Johnny Roach throws to him. Hank Gremminger goes up with Ron and tips the ball and Herb Adderley, coming up from left safety, grabs it.

"Damn!" Roach says.

"Way to go Hank and Herb!" Norb Hecker shouts. "Way to play that ball!"

It is the result of that tip drill he gives them. He pairs them off, the corner man and safety on one side, and he throws high to the corner man. The corner man tips it and the safety man takes it, and every now and then we get one just like this in a game.

Boyd Dowler goes down the right side from his flanker position on our 96. As Adderley comes across, Dowler gives him that good inside fake I asked for, then flies. But he has to slow down for Starr's pass and Adderley bats it away.

"Drop it over him, Bart," I say. "And don't wait so long until they get open."

Dowler was downfield 30 yards before Starr let it go, and by then Adderley had recovered. It is that conscientious conservatism of Starr. He wants to be sure the receiver is open, but he's got to anticipate it because, if he waits until he sees him open, that's make-up time for the defensive man. As it is, if he led him better he would still have con-

106

nected because, when Dowler makes that good feint and gets that one-step advantage, he has such long legs and such speed that it takes the defensive back three steps to catch up.

"Yes, sir," Starr says.

Dowler is 6-5 and 220 and at Colorado he was not only All-Big Eight quarterback but he was also his team's leading receiver. His father was a high school and junior-college coach. Boyd was hurdling when he was in the second grade. In college he ran the 100-yard dash in 9.9 and the high hurdles in 14.2, and he was the Packers third choice in 1959.

The first I saw of him was in rookie camp, and that first day he beat everybody but dropped the ball. The second day he began to catch a little and the third day he looked fine. Then he went to the All-Star camp, and word came from there that he wouldn't make it. They said he wouldn't catch in a crowd, or to his inside, and that he had no courage.

There are a couple of ways to test a receiver's desire, though, and you do it first in intra-squad scrimmage. Timid ends or flankers won't block those big, bullying linebackers, but Boyd stuck his nose in there every time. Then we threw to him across the middle, and when he got belted he got right up. We never saw him go down and in, then shy and look out of the corners of his eyes and listen for footsteps, so we knew we had a good one.

We needed to know this because in his first game he dropped a TD pass, and he dropped three in two games before he caught one. He caught thirty-two passes that first year, though, to lead our receivers, and he was an almost unanimous choice as the league's Rookie of the Year.

Max McGee, at the other side, is quick and a great actor on those fakes. Boyd is not as quick but his stride is deceptive, although his long legs handicap him a little when he is running with the ball in a broken field because they provide such a target. Boyd doesn't swear, smoke, drink or gamble, and on this club they call him Mr. Clean. He is serious, intense and highly intelligent, and he is not one of those receivers who overrates himself and thinks he can get open on every play. In practice, he says, he overconcentrates on catching the ball so that in a game, in all that traffic, it will be automatic.

"You also find out," he says, "that in a game, if you're wide open bad things go through your mind, so you try to concentrate more on the ball."

As a receiver must, he has made a complete study, from films and his own game findings, of every defensive man he has to face. But like those other receivers and those defensive backs he has those night thoughts going into a game. Before that 1961 championship game, he says, he saw himself against Erich Barnes over and over, and he caught three for 37 yards and a touchdown.

Dowler is great at spotting defenses, too, and he makes few errors in judgment. That recognition of the defense is difficult to teach, so it is difficult to learn, because those receivers must spot it on that first step across the line, at the same time that the defense is trying to disguise it.

"Your key," Tom Fears will tell them, breaking in the new ones, "will be the safety man and defensive halfback on your side. In the Zone they're going to play deep and not let you get anything behind them, so if the safety man pulls back and the halfback comes in, it's a Zone.

"In the Key defense, if our halfback is blocking they go back to help out deep. You know what your halfback is doing, and therefore if he's blocking and they drop back you know they're in a Key."

That is the beginning of it, but although you will see the same defenses over and over you will probably never get the same situation twice. You give them those basic defenses and your own formations and you tell them how to run their routes and you try, on the blackboard and on the field, to set up the different situations and how the enemy personnel will play it. You never get that defensive man in exactly the same position, though, and then your receiver has to think of that signal and of how to escape the linebacker who will knock his timing off—and then you've got that timing.

"That timing" is that 3.5 seconds your quarterback has to get the ball away. If he doesn't get it off by then, except for those occasions when you can give him maximum blocking on a try for a long one, his chances of success are minimal. We know, because we've had watches on it, so receivers must make their open interval between 2.5 seconds and 4 seconds. That's all they've got—1.5 seconds—and it's all the time your quarterback has to anticipate, but there's a sense some receivers have about getting open. Fakes can be taught automatically, but it isn't just position. It's position with the defensive man trying to recover, and with his legs crossed, and each receiver has to find his own way. It's the artist with his paint brush or the pianist or violinist with his instrument, and there's your creativity.

"How to go, Bart!" somebody says now. "Nice catch, Max!"

It is that turn-out, sideline pass that is as sure as anything in the passing game. Your end runs as if he's going to fly, and as the defensive halfback goes deep, he kicks out and changes direction to the sideline. He is out of the linebacker's reach, in an area that's difficult to cover. And if the end is in danger the quarterback can throw it over the sideline so it cannot be intercepted.

As the end comes off the line he has to be aware of the linebacker. If the linebacker starts to drop back and comes across at an interceptive angle, the end, instead of kicking out, must slide back in. If he does this he's open, and the fans think it's a different play.

"Run under that ball!" I'm hollering at Gary Barnes now. "Don't leap!"

It is a habit most of them bring out of college. They have got to run under the ball, rather than leap for it. While they're in the air they're losing time to gain on the ground, but it is only one of the mechanical problems we have to solve with the first-year men. If they are right-handed, if they've thrown a baseball with the right hand and caught it with the left, they catch better over the right shoulder, with their left hand as the major catching hand.

The ball, thrown by a right-handed passer, is revolving clockwise and away from them on that side, but over the left shoulder it is revolving toward them while the right hand becomes the major catching hand. They must acquire equality to both sides, and when they have to come in on the ball it is revolving counterclockwise as they grab it.

"Okay! Okay!" I call. "Let's go to our running game."

I call the defensive formations now, and the down-and-yardage situations. Starr and Roach run the plays I gave them in the coaches' room, and then our defensive men pull on, over their white Packer jerseys, sleeveless yellow jerseys with the numbers of our opponent's offensive players. I go over the defense, with Phil Bengston and Norb Hecker, and Red Cochran and Bill Austin, refer to the charts, have our offense run some of the other people's plays Phil and Norb have taken off the films and off Wally Cruice's scouting report.

"All right!" I say, after fifteen minutes of this. "Two-minute drill!"

Norb Hecker gets the two-minute stopwatch from Dad Braisher, and our defense gets out of the foreign jerseys. It is an end-of-first-half and end-of-game drill, and Norb holds the watch on it as I place the ball on the 20-yard line.

"Ball on our own 20!" I shout. "Two minutes to go. We need a touchdown to win. First and 10. Let's go!"

Sometimes I will tell them they need a field goal to win, and the drill is as good for the defense as it is for the offense. Now Starr hits Max McGee on a look-in over the line.

"All right!" I shout. "Second and 3. Hurry! Hurry!"

"Dapper! Dapper!" Ray Nitschke is shouting to Dan Currie. "Don't let 'em inside, Dapper!"

"Hurry! Hurry!" I'm shouting. "Let's go."

"Ball! Ball!" Nitschke is hollering now.

There are no time-outs, and Starr moves them down the field. At about the 45-yard line of the defense, though, Currie intercepts on a quick-turn-out to Ron Kramer.

"How to go, defense!" Phil Bengston hollers. "Way to play that, Dan!"

"Come on! Come on!" I'm shouting. "Everybody back. Let's go."

I place the ball back on the 20 and Norb starts the watch again. This time the offense goes all the way.

"One minute thirty-eight seconds," Norb Hecker says.

"Very good!" I shout. "That's all! Everybody up!"

It is twelve-thirty-six, but Willie Wood and Jerry Kramer remain on the field with Red Cochran. With Hornung still limping we may need Willie for kicking off and Jerry for field goals on Sunday.

"Don't keep them out too long, Red," I shout. Then I realize my voice is getting hoarse. It gets hoarse about this time every week, and in my first year I lost it completely during that first pathetic week in camp.

1:20 P.M.

I have had my hamburger and coffee. The defensive team has gone home. Red and Bill and Tom Fears and I are sitting in the darkened dressing room with the offensive team

110

watching the film of our opponent on defense two weeks ago against the Forty-Niners.

"You see that?" I say. "The fullback blocked left and the middle linebacker went to the side the fullback blocked on. As we've said, he keys on the fullback, except when they're in the Zone."

Somebody behind me kicks over an empty pop bottle and it rattles on the concrete floor. We've told them time and time again to put those bottles in the wooden boxes, and one of these days one of them, walking around barefoot or in just those white woolen socks, is going to get cut. They're like children.

"This is what they use all the time," I say as the Forty-Niners punt. "The 5-2, and they do a pretty good job of holding you up when you want to get downfield."

We watch the Forty-Niners sweep left. That 76, that 300-pound left tackle, is over the center in their Frisco.

"You see him over the center, Jim?" I say to Ringo. "He's a top-heavy guy, though, so all you have to do is take him low and he goes down."

It's the same problem I was discussing this morning with Bill in regard to springing Jimmy Taylor on our 22. Ringo is giving away seventy-five pounds, but he doesn't have to move that bull, just cut him down.

"Look at that third man in," I say as we watch them kick off. "That's the man the end has got to get. Ron?"

"Yep," Ron Kramer says.

"All right, they're in the Frisco now. Have in mind our 50, Bart. And how can it miss?"

"Yes, sir," Starr says.

"Look at the way their left end comes in deep on this one. That's why our 35-Cross will be good."

I want them to envision their own plays against these people, and I want them to envision them working. They must take the field with confidence or they just won't function, and this is one of the ways you build confidence.

"Okay," I say, looking at my watch and seeing that it's two-eleven. "That's all."

I take another crack at cutting our list of plays and then I get out of my sweatclothes and take a shower. Red Cochran is splicing back together our opponent's games with the Forty-Niners and the Colts. We've gotten all we can out of them by now, and the Forty-Niner game will go back to the other people and the Colt game will go to the Rams in Washington because they play the other people next week.

2:55 P.M.

I'm looking through my mail at the office and I find a letter from Wilmington, Delaware. I don't recognize the name signed to it or recall the others he mentions, but I remember that for part of a season I played guard for the Wilmington Clippers for $125 a game. I had that job with du Pont in the research lab and we practiced nights under the lights and played the Eagles and the Giants in those pre-season games.

Johnny Dell Isola was a guard with the Giants then. Like me, he was out of Fordham, and we met on the field during the warm-ups.

"We're both Fordham," he said, "so let's take it a little easy in there, Vince."

The first time they came off the ball he almost knocked me right up into the stands. Nineteen years later we got on the same side again, when he was coaching the Giants' line.

I pick up *Pro Football Illustrated*. I'm looking through it when I hear that spontaneous high laugh of Tony Canadeo. He was out of little Gonzaga in 1941, but for ten seasons he was a great back for the Packers. He set a club total-yardage record of over 4,000 yards gained that has stood all these years, although Jimmy Taylor may break it this season, and now he does a fine job experting our games on television with Ray Scott.

"How do you feel about it, coach?" he says, grinning.

"Well," I say, "I see in here that Tommy Harmon and George Connor pick us to win Sunday."

"It's nice to have the old pros on your side," he says, laughing. "You can't fool us old pros."

"I hope we can fool a few young pros," I say.

6:45 P.M.

Marie is feeling well enough to be up and around, so she will make that game on Sunday. She does not feel like going out for dinner, though, so Tim Cohane and I drive out to Manci's and Tim is talking about Jim Ringo and the Bears' middle linebacker Bill George.

In this league a number of genuine friendships spring up between opponents. They meet when they play together in the Pro Bowl Game, or they get to know each other during the off-season, and Ringo and George, who have been belting each other on that field for ten years, share a mutual respect and affection.

"When Ringo misses a block on George," I say, "George never lets him forget it. When Jim blocks him, though, you can hear George yakking at him all over the field."

"I'm sorry George was hurt on Sunday," Tim says. "I was looking forward to the duel. A year ago you beat the Bears here 24-0 but George was red-dogging through Ringo and Jim was like a kid pitcher who has won twenty-one games for Yale but has just been knocked out of the box by Harvard. His team wins, but he's absolutely desolate."

10:10 P.M.

Marie is watching television and I'm reading Art Daley's story in the *Green Bay Press Gazette*. He points out that between us and the other people we lead the league in thirteen of the sixteen defensive categories. Chuck Johnson has a similar statistics story in the *Milwaukee Journal* and Oliver Kuechle has a column comparing our strengths.

"Once again," he writes, "the immovable and the irresistible collide."

He writes that after three games we have the best rushing record in the league—an even 600 yards—and they have the best defensive record against rushing—203 yards. They have the best scoring record—119 points—and we have the lowest defensive yield—7 points. We have rolled up the most first downs rushing—34—and they have allowed the least—12. They have the best pass-completion percentage—64.6 percent—and we have allowed the lowest percentage of completions—46.1 percent.

"League history certainly offers little support for those who are now talking of an undefeated season along the banks of the Fox," he writes, and I am thankful for this. "Only twice since the league divided itself into Western and Eastern divisions, which was in 1933, has any team gone through the regular season without a licking. The Bears had 13-0 in 1934 and 11-0 in 1942, but both years lost the championship.

113

Washington beat them in the playoff in 1942, 14-6, and New York in 1934, 30-13.

"The immensity of achieving an undefeated season sometimes escapes the well-meaning enthusiast."

There is a lot that escapes that well-meaning enthusiast, without whom, of course, we'd be out of business. I think of something Dr. Anthony Pisani, who is head of orthopedics at St. Vincent's Hospital in New York, once said.

"The difference between you and me," he said, "is that millions of amateurs are looking at your X-rays."

I mentioned this once to Jim Nellen and Gene Brusky, our team physicians, and to Dr. Norman Erdman.

"That's right," one of them said. "You're being judged by amateurs while we're judged by operating-room personnel and a hospital staff of professionals."

"I'll tell you something else," Norman Erdman said. "For five years I worried before operations the way Vince does before a game, but after you've done a hundred gastrectomies or a hundred colectomies you know where, in almost all cases, those organs are going to be. They don't keep shifting on you like a defense does, and they don't fight back."

FRIDAY

7:49 A.M.

"We're late," Susan says.

We have met the yellow school bus, going in the other direction, opposite the St. Joseph Home for Children. We usually meet it up at the next corner.

"We're only a minute late," I say. "You'll be there in plenty of time."

Is she getting like I am, and my father before me? He is a precisionist, a perfectionist, if there ever was one, and when we were tearing out that basement under that two-story gray frame house in Sheepshead Bay and concreting the floor and ripping down those barns in the back we had to do it exactly his way. We got no weekly allowance and you had to earn your money with him, and while he was quick to criticize

114

he was quick to praise. When there was one of those violent scenes, though, he was not one to remember it any more than I am when I chew out a boy and fifteen minutes later can't tell you who it was.

"You see?" I say to Susan, stopping at her corner. "You had nothing to worry about."

"I know it," she says, and she has already had enough of me for the day. "Goodbye."

I can't remember, thinking of him, that my father ever watched me play at St. Francis Prep, but when I was at Fordham he became a real rah-rah. You had to win, though, and you got small sympathy when you didn't, and my fixation with the necessity of ignoring small hurts was his, too.

"No one is ever hurt," he would say. "Hurt is in your mind."

It was in my mind all right, I'm thinking while making the turn at that traffic light, but it was also in my mouth after that second 0-0 game with Pitt. It was on what Crowley called "The Halfback Inside Tackle." Andy Palau and I came out shoulder to shoulder. Tony Matisi took one step across that line and whup! whup! went those elbows. In the Polo Grounds dressing room later Doc Carroll put those thirty stitches inside my mouth. He was one of those short, quick, high-strung types like Doc Sweeney with the Giants, and when I got home that night I was certainly hurting in my mind.

8:32 A.M.

It is starting to mist when I come out of St. Willebrord's and it is still misting when I get to Sneezer's. Fuzzy Thurston is picking up a *Milwaukee Sentinel* at the stand outside, and I get one and go in and sit down.

Lloyd Larson has a column on the game, and he prints part of a letter from a fan which, he says, "is so typical of the spirit prevailing in this state at the moment." The fan picks us to win 36 to 13.

"The Pack is just too proud of its defense," the fan writes. "The defenders will have a record day, even blocking an extra point. They will, however, be surprised by a few startling plays. Still, I will pick the Packers and give 17 points without worrying a bit."

It must be nice to have no doubt, I'm thinking, but I hate

to see this kind of thing. They're all taking their line off that 49-0 game over the Bears last Sunday without taking into regard how hurt the Bears were coming in.

"Morning, Vince."

It is Phil Bengtson. He sits down next to me and opens his paper, and I go back to mine.

"That's what Vince Lombardi and his guys are up against these days," Lloyd Larson writes, and I'm glad to see this. "Fans have them on a pedestal. They are kings who can do so little wrong that the result is not open to question, regardless of opposition.

"That's a terrific vote of confidence, but fans' confidence will have no more effect than a drop of rain on a steel beam. The Packers have to prove their superiority, and that won't be easy. There is no law against that decisive victory, but judging by the records to date as well as the games between these two in the last few years, any winning margin, no matter how small, will be more than acceptable. I'm sure Lombardi, his staff and players, all realists, look on the game that way. They have been around too long to be lulled to sleep. They know every game is a dog fight, and that goes double when a big one like this comes along."

"Here's somebody," Phil Bengtson says, "who predicts we're going to block an extra point."

"I know," I said. "I saw it."

"He's almost got it right," Phil says. "Last night I guaranteed Bill and Tom that we'll block the first field-goal try."

I do not know what they are plotting, Phil and Norb, because I do not know what they have taken off the films on how our opponents block for their field goals. The psychological advantage you may derive from blocking a kick of any kind can take you all the way, though, if your offense just makes use of it. It is a great spot for the big bomb right on first down, although the other people know this as well as you do and, if they are not momentarily demoralized, they will be looking for just that.

8:55 A.M.

I walk through the dressing room and there are not as many of them here early today as there were yesterday. The game injuries are starting to heal and they don't require as much heavy taping. The only ones I see are our first-year men—Earl Gros and Gary Barnes, Ed Blaine, an offensive guard out of Missouri, Ron Gassert, a defensive tackle from Virginia, and Howie Williams, from Howard University. Howie couldn't quite crack our defensive backfield but he and Bob Jeter from Iowa, who played two years as a back in Canada, are on our taxi squad, meaning they are under contract, practice with us and can be activated if injuries deplete our regular squad.

Each year, out of the twenty we draft and the three or four free agents we bring to camp, we hope to get five, but we'll settle for four. Even if your squad is well balanced you want an offensive lineman, a defensive lineman, a back and a receiver, and would appreciate a promising defensive back, not to replace your regulars but to keep the squad young and rotating.

Our talent scouting starts with Dick Voris, our personnel director, and the roster of every college team in the country crosses his desk. Every senior is checked out by at least one of our sixty-five paid scouts, and we have an even greater number of friends who, in many instances, have done as good a job for us as the professionals.

Before the start of each season Voris sends each of our paid scouts two dozen forms on which to report on players he thinks have a chance of making it. A poor scout will fill out all of them before the season is over, but your best scouts send back only three or four. Your good scout will also recommend consideration of a lot of sophomores and juniors as well as seniors, while an inferior scout sees nothing in the still undeveloped sophomores and juniors and recommends only a lot of seniors.

In addition to our paid scouts and friends, Voris, Bill Austin, Red Cochran, Norb Hecker and Tom Fears scout, too. It is a scramble for them each weekend, because they can't leave here until practice is over on Friday and they must be back by Sunday morning, and this week Dick will be in Virginia, Bill at Michigan State, Red at Georgia Tech, Norb at Northwestern and Tom at Notre Dame.

Before the annual league draft meeting in early December we have our own staff meeting, and each of us has read all the reports on hundreds of players and we have privately graded each man. By our system a 1 to 5 rating means the boy should be a star in the league, 6 to 12 means he should make our squad, 13 to 22 means he should make some squad in the league and 23 to 30 means he shows enough promise to be brought to camp.

"I rate this boy 2," I'll say. "Why do you rate him 6?"

Out of this, out of all the arguments, we draw up our list of players. We know that every other team in the league has been looking at the same players and are probably coming to the same conclusions about most of them. But their needs are different from ours, so we discuss what we need.

Although our primary need, for the future, may be a defensive tackle, we are not necessarily going to put one at the top of our list as our number one or number two choice. Your first and second choices are going to be the best players you can draft, regardless of position, and you reason that each year there usually are only about thirty real good college players available. Because we are league champions, thirteen other clubs will draft ahead of us, but that still gives us two picks within that first thirty. If our need does happen to be a defensive tackle and there is one who is listed in our top thirty and we are lucky enough to get him we then accomplish two things. We draft a top-flight football player, and we fill a need.

Then we go to a hotel ballroom in one of the league cities, and we are there from 9 A.M. to 4 A.M. and they wheel in a buffet lunch and we adjourn only for dinner. Each club has its round table with the water jug and glasses on it and there is that table with a coffeemaker and cups off to one side. At one end of the big room there is a blackboard with the clubs listed in the order in which they will draft. And it is miserable when you draft fourteenth and have to sit there and listen while the others pick off the plums your own scouts and coaches have been watching and waiting for—in some cases, for three years.

So they start drafting and the names go up on the board next to the names of the teams and you start scratching them off your list. Once in a while they miss one, though, and then we sit there, a couple of our coaches, Dick Voris, Tom Miller and I, and we start second-guessing ourselves. He's in our first thirty and after two go-arounds he's still there. He survives the third round, so you get on the phone and you call his coach. Maybe he has a bad knee we know nothing about, or maybe he has already signed with the other league or in Canada.

I remember one year when it took the Colts an hour and a half to make a particular pick and everybody was up walking around and talking and needling them. Now they have that twenty-minute time limit, though, so you've got to get that information over the phone in a hurry.

118

The first three rounds go quickly, and then the process starts slowing as you begin playing checkers with players. You know not only your own needs but the needs of the other clubs, too, and you start to make calculated guesses.

"If we pick this kid on this fourth round," I'll ask the others at our table, "will this other boy still be available on the fifth?"

This other boy is, perhaps, an offensive guard we need more than we need the halfback. Now we go over the clubs ahead of us, the players they've already drafted, and their needs are still alive.

"I think these people may take him," one of our coaches may say.

"I doubt it," another may say. "They could use a guard, but they still don't have that end they need more. I think they'll go for this boy here at end."

So you gamble. For your fourth choice you take the half-back you don't need as much as that offensive guard. Then you sweat out that fifth round, waiting while those thirteen others pick, and you've invested over $50,000 and a lot of work in the scouting for those four or five you hope will end up making your squad this year. Now this offensive guard survives the tenth and eleventh and twelfth picks. On the thirteenth pick, just ahead of you, the Giants take him— or they don't. That's the gamble.

After the fifth round the tension begins to ease and while somebody else is making up his mind how he's going to if-bet on this pick, you start moving around the room. You stop off at another table to talk about something that has nothing to do with the draft, and they turn over their top-priority list and, if they're not well organized and have to have their records here, they turn those over, too.

From the fifteenth to the twentieth round it is just tedious. You have been at it now for seventeen or eighteen hours, with just the break for dinner, and you've smoked too many cigarettes and have had too many cups of coffee and you've lost your coaches. They have grabbed planes to try to sign the men you've already drafted and you've had other men standing by around the country and ready to go, too. Even so, you won't get them all, and last year we lost two choices to the other league because we were too late, but Dick Voris lived with Earl Gros for twenty-eight days and never left him until he signed him.

Now I walk by those first-year men, those five who survived out of the twenty we drafted and the four free-agents we brought to camp. I walk out the back door and through the mist to the head of the ramp leading down to the stadium field, and I see that Johnny Proski has the tarpaulins on, so in spite of this weather, and if we can just get a clear day on Sunday, it won't be too bad.

"How's it look?" Phil Bengtson asks when he sees me coming back through that door. "Like a duck pond?"

"Johnny has it covered," I say.

"Won't the sun ever shine again?"

"It will," I say, "if we win."

So you've drafted your first-year men and your people have signed them and by the time July comes you are like a kid waiting for Christmas morning. During the months since the draft your coaches, one after the other and as if to reassure themselves, have been repeatedly telling you about this boy or that boy they recommended, and you can hardly wait to see what you're really getting.

"What time did you say they'll start coming in?" I ask Dick Voris, probably for the third or fourth time.

"That plane is due in any minute now," he says, "and there should be ten of them on it. A couple of them are driving, and the rest will be in at the airport at six-twenty-five."

It is that first Sunday afternoon and we are sitting in the office on the first floor of Sensenbrenner Hall. It is so quiet in the dormitory that I can hear a faucet running somewhere, and in three days, when all the veterans are in, this place will be filled with noise. Jerry Kramer's hi-fi will be going and there will be shouting and singing and doors slamming, but outside the window now the campus is almost deserted, with only two nuns, here for the summer school, walking slowly along one of the paths in the sunlight.

"That must be the plane now," Dick says. "Hear it?"

I picked up the mimeographed roster again, once more I go over their names and their weights, and then, finally, we hear the taxis pull up outside.

"Here they are," Dick says. "For better or worse they're here, coach."

He gets up and goes out to meet them. I can hear them coming up the steps. Then he leads them into the office. They're carrying their luggage. He introduces them.

They're babies. They look so young. We drafted men and they look like boys, nervous and shy and afraid to squeeze your hand. Each year I know they're going to look like this to me, their faces soft and still unmarked by maturity, but each year I am shocked by that contrast with Dave Hanner, who, with that round face, must really have looked like a baby when he first appeared. And with Ray Nitschke, with his battle scars, and with Hank Jordan, who is fighting a losing battle to keep his hair and tries one restorative after another.

"I'm glad to meet all of you," I say, "and we're glad to have you with us. Dick Voris will assign you your rooms and fill you in on what you have to know before our first meeting this evening."

"Excuse me, coach," Emory Kroening, the photographer for the *Green Bay Press Gazette,* says, "but do you mind if we get a couple of pictures?"

Then he poses them, one of them shaking hands with me, and the others watching. If they want a pictorial memento of their experience in pro ball, I am thinking, they had better clip this picture tomorrow because unfortunately the rate of attrition will be so high that most of them are not going to make it.

Dick Voris gives them their room keys and they leave. This dormitory is finally beginning to come to life. In my mind I'm trying to match their faces with the names I've known for so long, but I have a feeling I won't remember them. That's going to be a problem during the next few days.

"Do you understand that, Jones?" I'll say in one of those evening meetings. "Where are you, Jones?"

The rest of them, first-year men and veterans, will laugh. I don't mean Jones, I mean Smith, because we cut Jones this morning and he's probably already back home.

"Well," Dick says when he comes back from getting them settled, "how do they look to you?"

"This boy's not a defensive end," I say, pointing to the name on the roster. "He's not rangy enough. Defensive tackle is where he's going."

"He's down for 6-3," Dick says, "and 245."

"He looks like he's 270," I say. "He's in terrible shape."

So many of those linemen think we want weight so they come in twenty-five pounds over, and it's all fat. There was that one we drafted a couple of years ago and he should have been 265 and he was 319. He took one lap around the field that first morning and I was afraid he was going to have a heart attack so I sent him home on the next plane. We had brought him a thousand miles and he had had two meals and one lap, and he probably never even saw his picture in the paper because Lee Remmel had to pull it out of the *Press Gazette* after the first edition.

"This boy here doesn't look too smart," I say to Dick. "How were his marks?"

"He didn't make any dean's list," Dick says, "but up here they don't have any books to worry about. All they've got to learn is football."

"I'm getting itchy," I say. "I want to get out there and look at them."

"Tomorrow, coach," Dick says. "Tomorrow's the day."

There are physical exams that first night, with the first-year men and the four or five veterans who check in early all lining up in the gym. There are six doctors, each behind a desk with the sign identifying his department: 1. History. 2. Heart-Lungs. 3. Dental. 4. Blood Pressure. 5. Abdomen-Hernia. 6. Eye-Ear-Nose-Throat. And I wish there were another one: 7. Desire. You can't examine them for that, though, and it shows only under game conditions or perhaps in contact work, which is why we start our contact drills on the second day in camp.

Usually they all pass, occasionally one of them doesn't. When the doctor tells you that you'd be taking an awful risk with one of your high draft choices it knocks you right into a cocked hat.

"All right, everybody!" you say in the dressing room the next morning. "Let's get down on that field and start with those three laps. Let's go!"

It is amazing how on that first day one or two impress you with the grace with which they move. Even before some of them put on a uniform you get that feeling from them. And then there's another one and you'll wonder why you ever brought him into camp. You have two reactions. First you feel an urge to work just on that good one, to see how perfect you can make him. But then you realize you must work on the others, too, in order to make a team, and so you spend most of the time you can give—and it's never enough —with the ones who lack natural ability, but whom you need.

And you must always fight the danger of personal involvement with them, because only one out of five is going to make it. It is hard enough to tell even a comparative stranger that you must cut him. And yet, try as you do to remain objective, to consider them only as ballplayers, they are young men out in the competitive world for the first time, and you know with what high hopes most of them left their homes and their friends and their towns to come here and make their try.

They were big men, too, in their colleges, but the size and reputation and polish of the veterans defeats them. When you pass them on campus or in the dressing room or on the field those first few days they nod, but they're still afraid to look you in the eye. In the dining room they sit apart and converse in low voices, and the only laughter comes from the coaches' table and the tables of the veterans.

At those "Rookie Shows" each dinner hour they stand up on those chairs, while the rest are eating, and they are so scared that, even if they have fairly good voices, they can hardly sing. The first night each of them usually attempts his college song, and the veterans, who had to go through this once themselves, boo them.

It is a carry-over, of course, of college hazing, but it has its purpose. On a ball club the veteran has many friends who instinctively resent the first-year man. If the boy is a back the veteran linemen might open the gates on him in scrimmage. If he's a lineman they'll put out harder against him. As a result the first-year man may be chased out of camp because of affection for a veteran who can no longer perform as well, and the team suffers.

When they boo them, then, and laugh at them at those dinner performances some of this resentment is expended right there, and if the boy takes it well and keeps trying the beginnings of new bonds start to form. After the fourth day the better ones have had a chance to express themselves on the practice field so they express themselves better in their acts, too. I remember how Howie Williams, after he had had a good day covering Max McGee, stood up there that night and did that Harry Belafonte number and surprised us all with his good voice and with his now almost professional elan.

"Here you go, Howie!" Lew Carpenter was saying to him on the field the next morning, tossing him a football. "Let's go!"

It helps all of them, even those who cannot sing well and those who cannot play football well enough to stay. After a week, when you pass them on the campus, they are giving you a smile and sometimes even a wink with their hellos, but if you are pretty sure by then that you are going to have to cut them this just makes it more difficult for you.

You have to tell them, though, one after another and eventually four out of five, and that first cut comes at the end of the first week. I remember one who was hoping to support four younger brothers and sisters by playing pro ball, and it is never easy. It is especially difficult after a boy has survived the first cut, and the second and the third, and he has been trying so hard. I have seen some of them who just couldn't keep the tears from coming into their eyes, but they still thank you for giving them the chance and they tell you it has meant a lot to them even though they failed. You tell them that you hope you have helped them, and that you will try to place them elsewhere in the league. Then you shake hands.

"This," I have said often, "is one of the hardest parts of this job." And cutting a veteran is even more difficult.

9:30 A.M.

I have changed into my practice clothes, and while the other coaches are talking about their travel arrangements for their scouting this weekend, I'm sitting at the desk looking over our ready-list of plays. I try again to rearrange the blocking on our Sweep against both the 6-1 and the 4-3, but I come back eventually to the way we've been doing it, and Bill Austin calls this "justifying himself."

"If you were going to Atlanta next week you couldn't get back for the game," Norb Hecker is saying to Red Cochran, and next week we'll be playing the Vikings away.

"Yes I could," Red says. "There's a di-rect flight leaves Atlanta at seven-thirty for Minneapolis."

"Notice he said 'di-rect,' " Phil Bengtson says.

"What's the matter with that?" Red says. "That's good Confederate English."

"Phil," I say, "out there today give me that other thing once in a while—the Frisco Strong, and give me that Blitz."

"Right," he says.

I walk into the trainer's room, and the last of them are having their ankles taped. I take three wheat-germ pills, as they're all supposed to do every day.

124

"And don't forget the citrocarbinate, coach," Bill Quinlan says. "We can't have you getting a muscle pull."

"I'm just worried about my vocal chords," I say. "Let's go."

On the blackboard in the dressing room Bill Austin has posted the honors for the Bears game and several of them are looking at them. When they see me come in they go to their dressing stalls and get their chairs and join the others who are waiting.

"This morning," I tell them, "we'll try to cut down a little. We'll have fifteen minutes on the running game, fifteen minutes on the passing game, fifteen minutes on defense and ten minutes on the goal line. We've got to work out there, but all that work isn't going to help us unless we're thinking, too. It's upstairs, upstairs.

"Now these other people are still talking. They're saying we beat the worst Bear team in history. They're not impressed by us, but you've always risen to the occasion, and the tougher it is the better you are. This is going to be a tough one, but that doesn't bother me in the least and it shouldn't bother you. All you have to do is play your game."

The backs and receivers stay with Red and Tom Fears in the dressing room and the offensive line goes into the coaches' office with Bill Austin. Phil and Norb take the defense into the visitors' dressing room, and I wander from group to group, listening to the coaches going over those same assignments again. In this game you must repeat everything often enough to reach the slowest member of your team because a single mistake can ruin the perfect work of ten others. The problem is to keep from boring some of those others. Dan Currie says he sees his assignments in his sleep.

10:20 A.M.

The mist has stopped when we go down to the field, but they are wearing their rain jackets again. They do their running and Jerry Kramer does his skipping. The quarterbacks and receivers and defensive backs start tossing balls back and forth, and Paul Hornung comes over to the ball bag by the camera tower.

"How's the thigh feel?" I ask him.

"It's not too bad today," he says, the worry gone from his face. "It feels a lot better."

He finds a ball. Bart Starr goes out to hold for him and he tries a few field goals from the 35-yard line. It's his left thigh, so it should not interfere with his kicking. I watch him take his steps. His right ankle is locked in walking position because if the foot is dropped forward the toes will hit the turf, and if the toes are up the heel will hit.

He puts three of them over and they move back to the 45-yard line. The first one he tries from there veers to the left so his left foot must have been too close laterally to the ball and his right foot must have hit the ball on the right side. You can tell from the squirting motion of the ball, the absence of that slow, even turnover, that he must also have hit too high up on the ball.

He makes a couple and I walk down to the other end where Red Cochran is watching Boyd Dowler and Max McGee punting upfield. Max rockets one out of there and then Boyd booms one a good 70 or 75 yards. He'll kick some 80-yarders for you, too, but about twice a season he'll kick 25 yards.

Red Cochran's theory about that is that Boyd's height has something to do with it. Yale Lary, of Detroit, is 5-10 and a great punter, but Boyd is 6-5 and has such long legs that the control of the free-drop of the ball from the hands to the foot is more difficult.

Yale Lary has another advantage, too, in that he plays on the defensive team. Both our punter and our place-kicker are on our offensive team and it's third down and 15 and Dowler has just run 30 yards on a pass route when he has to come back and punt. Hornung has the same problem, and people wonder why he sometimes misses from the 20-yard line but makes them from the 50. By the time we get to the 20 he's been in there for three or four first downs. If we're short on third down just across midfield he's not as tired, and so he's more accurate.

"Okay!" I shout now. "Let's go! Let's go!"

"Who leads?" somebody says, while they're forming by the tower for calisthenics. "How about Hawg!"

"Get up there and sound off, Hawg!" Ray Nitschke shouts at Hanner. "Take that chew out of your mouth so we can hear you."

We give them just two minutes of the calisthenics today and Willie Davis leads them around the far goalposts. We have them charge off the snap of the ball, and then the offensive and defensive lines go down to the end zone of the far field, and the receivers and offensive and defensive backs form two lines for the passing drill.

Bart Starr and Johnny Roach alternate throwing to them. They are too loose. They're running downfield with their hands dangling at their hips instead of being ready to reach up there for the ball.

"Come on! Come on!" I holler at them. "Let's carry our hands high!"

Ron Kramer goes down from the left line. He has that long, heavy, loping stride and he's holding his hands over his head and waving them as he runs to get under the ball.

"Showboat!" Jesse Whittenton hollers at him.

"Oof! Oof!" the rest are calling. "Oof!"

Kramer is 6-3 and at the end of last season weighed 250 pounds. That's big, even for a tight end, and that nickname —Oof—derives from Norm Van Brocklin's dismay last year. We were playing the Vikings in Minneapolis the next Sunday and I was talking with Van on the phone and he said, "Tell me something. Are you bringing that big oaf with you again?"

"How to go, Oof!" they're hollering at him now. "Oof! Oof!"

Ron Kramer is today the best tight end in the league, and yet that August of 1961 I was close to giving up on him. He had come here in 1957 out of the University of Michigan as one of their all-time greats—All-America end for two years and good at basketball and track, as a high-jumper and shot-put and discus man, too—and he had a fine first year here. In 1958 he had gone into the Air Force, and when I came here in 1959 and he got out of the service he looked like he'd be worth nothing. His legs were bad and his attitude was worse. It was the case of the great college star who had had an excellent first year but was now falling on his face. He became moody and sullen.

In 1959 and 1960 we carried him, but all that was saving him was his reputation and his potential. When camp opened in 1961 I was thinking of trading him because we could still deal on his reputation, while if we kept him for another season but didn't play him we'd ultimately get nothing for him.

I called him in, instead, and gave him his last chance. I told him I would start him in every pre-season game, but that if he didn't come through for us he was done. Paul Hornung and Ron were friends by then, and I think Paul did a lot to restore the big guy's confidence, because he started to look good right away, and today it scares me to think how close I came to quitting on him.

Your closed end has that big learning problem, but Ron was a psychology major at Michigan and he is intelligent, and on Thursday and Friday nights during the season he will be at Bart Starr's house, the two of them sitting behind the projector and studying the opponent's defenders. He's the physical ideal, too, which permits us to do things with our running game we could never do before he snapped out of his depression.

In the past our closed end used to double-team with our tackle in blocking. Ron is so big and so strong and so vicious a blocker, though, that he can wipe out a man by himself and, because this frees another blocker, it is almost like owning a permit to put twelve men on the field. Beyond that he has deceptive speed and great hands, and when he grabs that ball it is difficult for a defensive back to stop him, and I've seen him crumple a few big linebackers, too.

He still needs that pat on the back, though. He is sensitive and a worrier, and he is one of those who can't eat before a game.

"If I get up the day of a game and feel good," he says, "I'm especially worried. I mean if it's one of those days when all the world looks good to you and you're happy you feel like shaking hands with people instead of going out there and hitting them."

He's volatile, too, and I remember the time a linebacker grabbed his face mask. Ron turned around and, right in front of the official, kicked the linebacker in the shins, and that's why I was warning him the other day about this roughneck he's going to play against on Sunday.

"So it costs you 15 yards," he said after that incident, "but it stops those——. Too many ends let those guys get away with it. Not me."

Now we bring our defensive linebackers in and put them and our defensive backfield against our passing stuff. I watch while Bart Starr, dropping back, looks toward Gary Knafelc, who is in at closed end now. He finds him covered by Dan Currie and hits Gary Barnes, coming across on a slant. This is exactly what I told Starr about taking a look at that quick man first.

"That's the way, Bart!" I'm shouting. "Very good!"

"Double-Wing!" Ray Nitschke is calling. "Double-Wing!"

"Not so loud!" I holler.

I watch Starr hit Jimmy Taylor over the line. Then he throws to Ron Kramer on that sideline pass to the right.

"Ball! Ball! Ball!" Nitschke is hollering, and when Kramer grabs it in front of Herb Adderley, "Damn!"

Boyd Dowler goes downfield now and makes the right-angle turn of the Square-In. He hesitates, though, and the ball bounces off his fingers.

"Don't stop there!" I'm hollering. "Don't hesitate!"

The quarterback has it tough enough as is. Dowler's stride is different from McGee's and Ron Kramer's and Gary Knafelc's and Gary Barnes', and each has his own way of making his fakes and running his routes, and Starr has to assimilate all that. For him to anticipate the receiver correctly that receiver must commit himself freely in his customary and natural style.

We bring the offensive and defensive lines into it now. Starr and Roach mix running plays in with the pass plays, and after fifteen minutes of that I move the ball down to the 6-yard line.

"All right!" I say. "Third and 6 to the goal line. Let's go!"

For ten minutes they run our goal-line plays. Then I move it out to the 20-yard line and go behind the defense and watch the last five minutes of it from there.

It is eleven-thirty now and the offensive team puts on those sleeveless yellow jerseys with the other people's numbers. Hornung quarterbacks one backfield and Lew Carpenter the other and Red Cochran has the charts of the other people's pass plays. While one backfield is running one play the other backfield is studying the chart of the next play.

"Ball! Ball! Ball!" Nitschke is hollering.

Johnny Symank, who is really a defensive back, is wearing number 41 and imitating the opponent's flanker. He runs a Square-Out, and as Herb Adderley cuts over to cover him their feet become tangled. Symank, like the others, is wearing a helmet but no pads, and now I see him flying through the air and right for that camera tower. He hits the ground about 2 yards from it, somersaults and ends up between the legs of it.

We're all watching him now, and he scrambles up and comes running back. He is only 5-11 and at 180 pounds he is the lightest man on this squad. Compared with the others he looks like a baseball infielder, but he is a football player. The Packers drafted him out of the University of Florida in 1957 and that year he was fourth in the league in interceptions. Last year he had the highest interception-return yardage and best kickoff-return average on this club.

"Showboat!" somebody is hollering at him now. "Actor! Actor!"

There is no actor in Symank. He is serious and intense, and in a game he'd just as soon break your leg as not. He has made it in this league because he gets a great deal more out of himself than his ability and size justify, and I wish I could say this about all the rest of them. Many of them will rise for one game or two, but John gets the maximum out of himself in every game, and if I had thirty-five others like him I'd have a far better team than I have.

"I stopped in at the Symanks," Marie was telling me one night a year or so ago. "They have that new house but there's no lawn in yet. With all that mud outside and those four little ones running in and out that house was still so clean that I was so ashamed I came right home and started to clean here."

Now it is eleven-forty-five and a fog is starting to settle over the field, but we got in what we wanted and I send them in. Only Willie Wood stays out, practicing kickoffs with Norb Hecker. At 5-10 and 185 he doesn't have all the power you want in your kicker, but as our free safety on defense he's great to have back there on kickoffs, too. He's an instinctive, vicious, secure tackler, and now he's got to remember not to let his approach get him too close to the ball. If you lack power your tendency is to run at that ball harder and to try to murder it. If your left foot is closer than 18 inches you have to elevate the right leg more than is natural and you don't meet the ball as you must to get that slow turnover. The height to go with the distance comes from your power and leg drive, and rhythm will come from your follow-through.

11:55 A.M.

The players are taking showers and I'm sitting at the desk looking again at the other people's roster to be sure I've got all those jersey numbers in mind. Bill Austin is rewinding film on one of the projectors.

130

"You know," I say to him, "this is probably the biggest game of the year and they were as loose as a goose out there today."

"That's still better than being all tightened up," he says. "They'll be all right come Sunday."

I walk into the trainer's room. Paul Hornung is lying on his back and Bud Jorgensen is going over those left thigh muscles again with the diathermy.

"How is it now?" I say.

"It's not bad," Hornung says.

"How's Moore's shoulder?"

"It's come around real well," Jorgensen says. "He says it feels good now."

When the rest have finished showering and have dressed, Bill Austin moves out the blackboard with their performance percentages in the Bears game on it. They sit down, and we have our Honors Assembly.

"Now last Sunday," I say, "we had by far our best blocking day offensively. Max McGee, that was 100 percent improvement over the week before."

"How to go, Max!" somebody says.

"But, Max," I say, "we're going to need that again this week."

"I'll be tryin'," Max says.

"I know you will," I say. "Ron Kramer, twelve blocks for 71 percent and an award."

"Oof! Oof!" they are shouting.

"Dowler, three for three and 100 percent and an award."

"Way to go, Boyd!"

"Jimmy Taylor, ten for 45 percent. You've got to do better, Jim."

"I know," he says.

"Elijah Pitts, nine for 40 percent. Wrong techniques. Blaine, nine running for 40 percent. Barnes, one for 100. Skoronsky, 82 percent on running plays, 87 percent passing and an award."

"How to go!"

"Jim Ringo, 74 running and 86 passing for an award. Jerry Kramer, 86 percent on runs, 100 percent on passes and an award. Gregg, 87 percent and 100 percent passing and an award. Willie Davis, an award for tackling the passer. Ray Nitschke, for a tackle inside the 20 on a kickoff. Ron Kramer for a run over 20 yards and a TD. Willie Davis for tackling the passer again. Elijah Pitts and Ken Iman for tackling inside the 20 on a kickoff. Hank Gremminger for a pass interception. Willie Wood for a pass interception. Dave Hanner for tackling the passer. Nitschke for an interception. Herb Adderley for an interception and for a run over 20 and a TD.

"Now that's it for last Sunday," I tell them. "I want to see that same thing again this Sunday, with the rest of you people in on it, too."

It is what Gary Knafelc calls "the old incentive plan, like the star on your report card." He is also the one who said, "Lombardi works you so hard that, when he tells you to go to hell, you look forward to the trip."

Knafelc backs up Ron Kramer at closed end and, while he doesn't have Ron's bull strength in blocking, going for that ball or running with it, he has great hands and has made some sensational catches in his eight years with this club. He and Bart Starr are buddies, rooming together in training camp and on the road, and he is a handsome guy who, Marie says, looks like Gardner McKay. He is an excellent after-dinner speaker, has his own local television show and he says that some day he'd like to write a book about this game.

"When you play pro football," he says, "you're two people. You're the animal on the field, and off it you're a reasonably intelligent, well-mannered family man. When you're a rookie you're worrying about every squad cut. Then for five or six years you're secure, but as you get older you find yourself worrying again as you did when you were a rookie. It isn't the physical torture—you can put up with that if you know you're going to make the club—it's the mental torture.

"Then you've got those pre-season intra-squad scrimmages. Believe me, I'd rather play the Bears and the Lions back-to-back than go through one of those. You may be trying to beat a friend out for the same position. Even if you're not you've got to go out there and take those blind-side shots at people you've worked with and socialized with for years because your livelihood, your security, depends on it. There's nothing personal about it but it does something to you. You wonder what kind of person you are."

Now we've got the offensive team watching once more that 17-13 loss to the other people in the season opener last year. I have been yakking at them all week and I want them to see it for themselves, so I am not going to say much except to point out a few things that may help to make them believers in the plays we are concentrating on for this game.

"Now that's a pretty good example of what that 47-Out-side will do for you," I say after Moore has picked up 8 yards on it. "See it, Bart?"

"Yes, sir," Starr says.

"Now the reason we didn't get more on this," I say, watching a pitchout to Hornung, "is that they had the blitz on. That's why this week we're doing what we are with the split end. You fly! Right, Max?"

"Right," McGee says.

"Max will take that safety man who came in to tackle Hornung deep with him on that Fly."

We watch in silence while the other people score. Then Starr starts to hit McGee and we move it down to where they stop us once more and Hornung kicks the field goal as the reel runs out.

"You see that, Max?" I say. "You run that 6-pattern, and you can break them wide open again."

"I know," McGee says.

From the 50-yard line that 28 of theirs kicks dead on our 2-yard line. Once again I have to watch while we spend the rest of the afternoon trying to get out of there.

"You see that, Jimmy?" I say to Taylor. "You ran a little wide here. See the good hole inside?"

"Right," he says.

Now we show the second half of our return game with them in their own ball park. We held them to three field goals in that one and outscored them 10 to 3 in that second half and beat them 17-9. Our real work for the week is done now and we'll see no more films. This is the picture I want to leave in their minds.

"Now this is exactly the same team," I say, "and we kept them out of there all day on the blitzing."

It was played in the mud, as this one may be on Sunday, and we watch as we go down there twice. Jimmy Taylor goes over from the 1, and Hornung kicks the final field goal. I snap off the projector.

"That's all," I say.

3:55 P.M.

I have had a sandwich and coffee at my desk at the office and looked through the mail and answered some of it. I have driven to the Northland Hotel for a haircut and I'm sitting in one of the chairs, the barber starting to work on me but not bothering me with Packer talk. My first year here I couldn't step outdoors without somebody wanting to talk about football, but happily they have learned that I am here to win games and not to entertain the populace with anecdotes and opinions.

"Afternoon, coach," somebody says.

"Hello, Forrest," I say. "How are you?"

"Just great," he says.

This is another real football player, this Forrest Gregg. He's a big Texan, 6-4 and 230 and out of Southern Methodist University, and I'll never forget what he did for us last year. He was as responsible as any of them for our success, because when Jerry Kramer's leg was broken in mid-season I had to move Forrest, my All-Pro offensive tackle, in at guard. He had played it one season, four years before, but he had to relearn those assignments, those pulling steps—the cross-over to the right and the throw-out to the left—and he had to master again that knack of running at full speed, like a back, and finding that hole.

He made no complaints, though, and he did an excellent job. My only regret is that it cost him a position on some of those newspaper All-Pro teams.

"That's all right," he said. "I think winning the championship was payment enough."

That's the way he is, a team player who, if he has any selfish thoughts, puts them aside. He expects this of all the others, too, and I've seen him, with that quick temper, flare at some of them in practice, but he's also got the laughter and the tears.

Marie calls Forrest a picture ballplayer and that's what he is. Watching him perform, watching him execute those assignments, you get that good feeling, and he has all the requisites. He's big enough and, although he's not quite as strong as either Bob Skoronski or Norm Masters, at the other tackle, he's strong enough, and he handles people like Gino Marchetti of Baltimore, Jim Houston of Cleveland and Lamar Lundy of Los Angeles, who are some of the best defensive ends in this league.

He's a fine downfield blocker, too. His speed isn't great but he's very quick off that ball and he has that mental sharpness to adjust quickly to sudden situations. He has that knack of getting in front of the runner and, with his excellent sense of timing, of making the key block.

134

When you combine all this in an offensive tackle with his ability, and willingness to play guard you've got quite a man. In this league it's very important for a team to have this versatility as insurance for when those injuries start piling up. In addition to the tackle who can play guard you should have at least one guard who can play offensive tackle and an offensive lineman or a defensive linebacker who can play center if necessary.

"Actually I like to play in the mud occasionally," Forrest is saying now, talking to one of the other customers waiting for a haircut. "I really don't know why, but I'll bet 75 percent of the guys would tell you that. Just once in a while it's kind of fun."

"But doesn't it get into your mouth and your eyes?" the other is saying, and I am reminded of that great picture of Gregg that Bob Riger took. It was during that game in the mud in San Francisco in 1960 when we beat the Forty-Niners 13-0, and Forrest looks like he is cast out of iron.

"It doesn't really bother you," Forrest is saying. "It gets in your mouth a little, although you try to keep it closed at the right time. It seldom gets in your eyes."

On the way home I drive out Washington Street. It is one-way and I am in the left lane. They are ripping up the corner at Cherry Street and, as I try to ease out, the light blue car on my right tries to keep me in. We both stop for the light and I see now that the other driver recognizes me. When we start again he is most considerate and waits while I move over ahead of him, the perfect, spurious gentleman.

6:45 P.M.

"On Monday, Tuesday and Wednesday we don't talk," Marie has said. "On Thursday we say hello. On Friday he is civil."

Marie and I have driven out to the Stratosphere for dinner and I am civil. We talk about the tea Marie gave for the team wives on Tuesday, but I'm thinking about their husbands. So far this season I have been worried about them carrying that burden of the title and being too tense, but they were so gay out there today that now I'm worrying about them being too loose.

"They'll be up for it," Marie says. "Stop worrying about it."

Paul Hornung comes in with his mother, and they stop

at our table. She is a pert, gay, delightful little lady of whom we are very fond and she is enjoying every moment of Paul's success.

"You're going to be my left halfback, period," I told him that first day in training camp. "The only way you can get out of it is to get killed."

Few things in this life work out so well. From an occasional quarterback, occasional halfback and occasional fullback he became last season not only the most valuable player on this club but in the league, and now he makes as much from those TV commercials and those ads as he gets for playing.

"Your mother and I are completely confident," Marie is saying to Paul now, "but we'll still have the nervous shakes. You know, I envy people who know nothing about football. When Vince had the high school team I'd sit with the mothers and one of them would say, 'Isn't Phillip doing well!' Actually, Phillip was doing everything wrong."

"I'll try to do everything right," Paul says. And he's blessed with that great smile, too.

9:45 P.M.

Art Daley has his Friday note column in the *Press Gazette* surmounted by pictures of the other people's two big defensive tackles and their quarterback. He quotes Wally Cruice as saying that the other coaches had trouble getting their club up for Baltimore last Sunday because they were already looking ahead to us. In the *Milwaukee Journal* Chuck Johnson writes that we'll both be in fine physical shape and he quotes the other coach as saying, "From watching the Packers in the movies I'd say they're certainly every bit as good as last year, maybe better. Can you imagine anyone beating the Bears, 49-0—and without Hornung in the line-up?"

Nothing I can do now is going to help us, so for the first time this week I can turn on television and be conscious of what's happening on the screen. Buddy Hackett is on the Jack Paar show and he is telling a story about his wife waking him in the middle of the night to go out in the snow to buy a pizza. In the middle of Buddy's story the phone rings and Marie answers it.

"The answering service," she says when she comes back.

136

"The nuts are starting—somebody in Philadelphia, somebody in Milwaukee and a woman and a man in Green Bay I've never heard of."

SATURDAY

7:45 A.M.

By Saturday, if we have not solved the problems that started accumulating on Monday, it is too late to worry about it, and so, driving into town I am aware of the scenes around me for the first time in a week. In the orchard on the right the apples are still green but in the field next to the children's home the purple cabbages are ready for picking. The leaves on the elms that line the street are all yellow now, and the fog is still with us although it is not as heavy as when we drove home from dinner last evening.

As I come out of St. Willebrord's, Dr. Gene Brusky is sitting in his car, parked in front of mine. When he sees me cross the street he gets out, and I wonder if he wants to play some golf this afternoon.

"I saw your car," he says, "so I thought I'd wait and tell you that Jim Taylor is running a temperature."

Oh, no, I'm thinking. Not Jimmy.

"What's the matter with him?" I say. "The flu?"

"Maybe," Gene says, "but he's not too bad. He called me last night and I went over to see him about nine-thirty. His temperature was 102, but luckily he didn't have a sore throat. I gave him some medication and I just came from checking on him. He's 101 now, and he feels pretty good. His throat is still all right, but I told him to stay on the medicine."

"What do you think?"

"He won't be out to practice today, but he'll be able to play tomorrow."

"You really think so?"

"I do," Gene says. "What I've given him should knock it out of him, and I'll check in on him again this afternoon and let you know."

137

Not Jimmy, I'm thinking while driving. You can't lose a fullback like Jimmy Taylor and not be hurt. Every week it's somebody, but Gene says not to worry and there's nothing I can do about it.

At Sneezer's I pick up the *Milwaukee Sentinel* and sit down at the counter. I open the paper to the sports page. Bud Lea's story is a final evaluation of the two teams.

"The teams are precisely matched," he writes, "although their talents differ in some ways. The powerful Packers establish their ground attack to set up their passing while the visitors use their passing to open up the defense for their running. The Packers will smash away methodically with the brutal running of Jim Taylor and Paul Hornung. . . ."

If we have Jim Taylor, I'm thinking. And even if we have him, will he have his strength? Play or not, though, it can't be as bad as 1959. We had won our first two that first year, to everybody's surprise, and Jimmy was at home and his wife was frying potatoes when they caught fire. Jimmy was padding around the house in his bare feet, and when he picked up the frying pan the fat spilled. He reported on Sunday saying he could play, but he couldn't get his shoes on and he was out for six games. All I could think of then was the year I had that good basketball team at St. Cecilia and we had a streak going when that star forward of ours picked up a hot plate and reported the night of the game with both hands bandaged. We won the championship but every year and every game it's somebody or something in this business.

The other coach, it says in Bud Lea's story, is more of a gambler than I am, and up to now a successful one. We're back to that again, because last Sunday and ahead only 42 to 0 I didn't go for the fourth-down yardage.

"Lombardi risks nothing," it says. "His team is the soundest in the business. It beats down an opponent with superior blocking and tackling."

Isn't that what football is all about? All your effort in any business should be directed to taking the risks out of it. If you don't believe that, give up on what you're doing and play the horses. Maybe if I had a quarterback who is more of a gambler I'd gamble more, but you fit your game to the talents and personality of your team as well as to your own and I've got a quarterback whose big card is his consistency. Besides, if you can hit the other people where they're strongest and break them there it's all over. It's like Bobby Layne says. He says everybody who plays us knows what's coming but that they can't stop it anyway.

"Somebody's winning streak has to give Sunday," Bud Lea writes. "But in Green Bay don't bet against the Packers."

9:02 A.M.

Most of them are already in the dressing room, getting out of their street clothes and into their sweatsuits. In the coaches' room Phil Bengtson is charting on white cardboard, using a plastic template and a French curve, one of the other people's plays. When he finishes, he works on rearranging our punt-return team.

Each time we send in that team we also send in word that we want a right or a left return. Up the middle is the shortest way to that other goal line but on the punt return, unlike on the kickoff return, the defensive line is right on top of you and you can seldom get that center of the field. On the kickoff return you've got time to form a wedge and take advantage of the better blocking. On the punt return, where they're up so close and the kick has a higher arc, you must often lose yardage to gain yardage, and you generally return outside not only because you can't count on getting the middle but also to give your blockers time to set up your screen.

For that screen you can use a minimum of three men or a maximum of five, and you tell them to get outside the colors, meaning the other jerseys. You have to put two men on the end covering the punt, because he definitely is not supposed to let anyone get outside of him, but before you can flank them you've got to hold up their coverage on the line of scrimmage. You can send in the maximum of nine men as potential kick-blockers, as the Bears do to make their opponent stay there and block, and forget your screen. But whatever you do you've got to have a safety man with sure hands and the judgment to know when to catch, fair-catch or let roll, and he has to have a lot of guts, too.

"So if he fakes and runs," Phil says, meaning their punter and showing it to me, "we'll be just as good."

What Phil has done is to penetrate the outside men, so instead of being the first to leave and form the wall, they are the last. A year ago, in that season opener, their kicker pulled it down and ran 14 yards with it, and we don't want him hurting us like that again.

I walk into the trainer's room and Tom Moore is having heat applied on his left shoulder. The others are being taped, or waiting until Bud Jorgensen and Dominic Gentile can get to them.

"You'd think this was the championship game," Tom Miller is saying, watching Jorgensen tape Jerry Kramer's right ankle. "The other people say they could have sold two thousand more seats if we had them."

In the equipment room four or five of them are ganging up on Dad Braisher, wanting cleat changes or new shoelaces. He has been equipment manager for the Packers for seven years and before that he coached at De Pere High School for thirty-three years and he is used to catering to the whims and eccentricities of athletes.

"Does anyone know if they've got the tarpaulin off?" I ask.

"Yes," Ken Iman says. "John is raking the strip down the middle."

"Why?"

"The high school band must have been playing up and down like they were on a track," Iman says. "It's pretty beat-up."

"They played here last night?"

"That's right."

Great, I think. They're talking of our game as if it's for the championship. You can't get a ticket for it and millions will watch it on television. All over the country they'll be waiting for the result, and the high school, instead of playing on its own field, comes out here and turns this one into a mudhole.

"How are you, Forrest?" I say to Gregg. "How's the haircut?"

"Fine, coach," he says.

"It's about time," somebody else says.

"It'll only grow again," Forrest says.

"All right," I say. "Let's speed it up so we can get out there."

At nine forty-five we go out and down the ramp and into the stadium. The turf isn't bad along the sides but inside the hashmarks and between both 30-yard lines the damp, soft dirt is almost bare of grass. The fog has lifted, and two of Johnny Proski's grounds crew are completing the repainting of the lines.

"These ballplayers are spoiled," Bill Quinlan is announcing, "When I was a kid I used to play on rock piles."

The defense have their white jerseys on and the offense the green. Paul Hornung is practicing field goals and Quinlan, Dave Hanner and Jim Ringo are fooling around, trying to drop-kick the ball over the crossbar from about the 20-yard line.

"Hey, Doc!" Quinlan shouts to Dr. Jim Nellen when Jim, who played tackle for Wisconsin, drop-kicks one back. "I thought you only used that old round ball."

"Not me," Jim says. "I'm too young."

"Not the coach, though," Quinlan says. "The coach used to play with the old round ball—the old Seven Blocks of Granite."

"Have you got enough, Paul?" I call to Hornung.

"One more," he says.

"Where's he kicking it from?" I say. "The 50?"

"The 52," Jesse Whittenton says, meaning from the farther 48-yard line.

Hornung lifts one and it has that good turnover and height and distance. It barely clears the crossbar and the others cheer.

"One more," Hornung says.

"Showboat!" somebody hollers.

Boyd Dowler is punting back toward midfield. He boots one high, and a good 60 yards.

"Perfect," I say to him. "That's the kind we'll be down there sitting under."

I have been trying to convince him to take 10 yards off the distance in order to get the height. The distance doesn't help much if it rockets down there before your speed-burners can get down under it.

"Even better, Boyd," I call on the next one.

His third one slides off the right side of his foot. It squirts no more than 30 yards before it bounces across the sideline.

"Back to normal," Ron Kramer says.

"Tarp! Tarp!" someone is hollering.

Johnny Symank has been chasing the ball. He gets down on his hands and knees and crawls over the open tarpaulin between the sideline and the stands so that his cleats won't puncture it, and some of the others bark at him and howl like hound dogs.

"All right!" I shout. "Let's get started!"

Jim Ringo, our offensive captain, and Bill Forester, our right linebacker and defensive captain, lead the men in calisthenics. They lead them on the day before a game and on the day of a game. Jim and Bill have been on this club together now for ten years. Each in his own way is a fine field leader, and where Ringo will occasionally flare at someone who is not doing his job, I have yet to hear Forester raise his voice or chew out anyone.

In fact I would say that there is no one on this club who is more quiet and self-contained than Bubba, as they call Forester. He is highly intelligent and steady on and off the field and his leadership is one of action rather than words. There is an aura of efficiency about him that the others respect and rise to, and I remember how, in my first year here, he turned two ball games around for us.

The first was that Thanksgiving Day game with the Lions in Detroit. In the second half they were starting to roll over us when Bubba broke through and dropped Earl Morrall, their quarterback, for a 20-yard loss, and after that they never recovered. In our last game of the season we were 14-14 in the third period at San Francisco when Bubba ran right over one of their halfbacks and threw Y. A. Tittle for a safety. That broke the game open and we beat them 36-14.

All linebackers have to have good size—and Bubba is 6-3 and 225—because they must be big enough and strong enough to shed the blockers and to stop a runner like Jimmy Brown. They must also be mobile enough to defend against the pass. The outside linebackers become, in effect, defensive halfbacks against the pass and defensive ends against running plays. The basic 4-3 defense is a 6-1 as the players line up, but it is a 4-3 in action because, unless they are blitzing, the outside linebackers don't go in. They play on the line of scrimmage and drop off when the pass shows, and the good ones who can handle this dual responsibility are hard to find.

Bubba, though, comes from a football family. His father played the game and coached in Dallas for eighteen years, and there is a stadium there named after him. Bubba and his older brother Herschel went to Southern Methodist, and later Herschel became a guard with the Browns. The Packers had Bubba at fullback, at guard and at tackle before they moved him to linebacker. He has been named All-Pro four times.

As quiet and composed as he is, though, Bubba can be reached and he'll rise for a game. He says he'll never forget that dressing room speech I made before the first game that first year. I'll never forget it either, because this was a team that had won only one and tied one the previous year and I had pushed them hard in training and now I wanted that win over the Bears to break our losing habit and to convince them that this was a new era. I didn't know how far I could go in trying to elevate them emotionally.

"He ended it," Bubba says, "by yelling, 'Go through that door and bring back a victory!' I jumped up and hit my elbow. That was my worst injury of the year."

After calisthenics we have them drive off the ball and then go into a skeleton passing drill against the linebackers and the defensive backfield. As Hornung goes out for a pass the draw string in the waist of his sweat pants becomes untied, but he grabs the pants with one hand and the ball with the other, and they whistle at him.

"How to go, Barnsey!" I shout.

Gary Barnes, with a good Zig-In and a change-of-pace, has got a step on Jesse Whittenton. As I watch, though, he drops the ball.

"You're making real good moves now, Gary," I tell him when he comes back. "You know it takes every bit this long."

"I know," he says.

"That's right," I say, "so don't be worrying about your moves from now on. You've got those, so concentrate on catching that ball."

"Yes, sir," he says.

Bart Starr arcs a long one to Gary Knafelc down the right. Knafelc, running hard, can't quite reach it and, before he can stop, he is on the tarpaulin.

"Tarp! Tarp!" the others have been hollering, and Knafelc tiptoes off it.

In Boyd Dowler's first year here Bart threw Boyd one like that in practice. When Boyd caught it he was going at full speed across the sideline and, as the rest of us watched, we suddenly froze because he was no more than 3 yards from one of those big steel tarpaulin cylinders. In that second we forgot that he had started hurdling in the second grade, and then he took one more step and cleared the cylinder in perfect form. He fell on the other side but he rolled over and got up smiling, and it was such an amazing feat that the rest of us just broke into spontaneous cheers.

"That's going to be a good pass," I'm telling Starr now, as Knafelc comes back. It is a Zig-Out route in which the tight end makes a three-step fake to the inside and then runs a corner.

"Was that all right?" Starr asks Knafelc.

"Sure," Knafelc says. "I'd have had it but I slowed for that tarp."

"All right!" I shout. "Bring them up. Let's go!"

Off to the right the offensive and defensive lines have been walking through their assignments. Now they line up so that we can run through just once more, and for the final time, some of the plays we have put in this week.

"Now give me a 5-1," I say to the defensive team, "and make the same deals from it."

By this I mean that the middle linebacker will line up directly behind the tackle over the center, and he will blitz to either side with the tackle hitting the opposite gap.

"That shouldn't bother you any," I say to Jim Ringo, meaning that he works with the guards against this defense and blocks area rather than a specific man. Therefore it doesn't matter how they deal.

"Uh-uh," he says, shaking his head.

"All right," I say. "Now give me the 4-4 both ways."

I want them to blitz both inside linebackers, first blitzing inside with the tackles looping out and then outside with the tackles slanting in.

Starr passes to Lew Carpenter. Lew, trying to get clear of Hank Gremminger, drops the ball.

"What was that?" I call to Phil Bengston.

"Strong," Phil says.

"Give it back to me again," I say to Phil, "and then give me the 4-3 with the linebackers in and the tackles going either way."

I mean I want the defensive tackles to slant right or left, with the weak-side linebacker and the middle linebacker blitzing through the area vacated by those tackles. Ringo has to pick up the middle linebacker wherever he goes, and both guards stay with the tackles.

"And we'll use our Backs Divide," I say, "but we'll pick up those linebackers if they blitz. Got that, Paul? Tom?"

"Right."

"All right," I say, and we have been out now for a half hour. "Kickoff! Let's go!"

Our kickoff team lines up on the 40-yard line. Each week we rearrange them according to how our opponent uses its

144

personnel and designs its returns. All I want our men to do now is to take their positions on that line so there will be no confusion tomorrow.

"All right!" I call. "Kickoff return."

They distribute themselves now from the 40-yard line back to the goal line. Our center, in the middle, is to knock down the other people's kicker, and Kenny Iman does a good job of that. Our two guards, on either side of him, are to drop back and then crisscross. They are responsible for the first man lined up on either side of the kicker, and by having them cross you are giving them the angle they need to drive those men to the outside. Our two ends are wide on the 30-yard line and they are to loop back and in, and then drive the two men who are third out from the kicker to the outside. On the 20-yard line we have three big tackles to form the center of our wedge. Behind the middle tackle is our fullback. If the kick is to our right safety man the fullback will move to his right and outside the tackle on that side. The left safety man will complete the left side of the wedge. If the kick is to the left safety man the fullback moves to the left and the right safety man moves up to flank the right side. The receiver is to follow that wedge until he sees an opening, and your safety men know that any kick that goes deeper than 5 yards into the end zone is to be left there, but only after it has been picked up. The exception is that they may run it out if it is a low kick and there is still a lot of daylight showing between those tacklers charging downfield.

"All right!" I say now. "Just remember that they leave a gap in the middle and the third man out is the first man downfield. If we can cut him down, Ron Kramer, and cross-block the middle we can have a good return."

"Right," Kramer says.

Our punting team lines up next in that spread formation. Boyd Dowler—or Max McGee, if he's our punter—is back 15 yards, and we've had the stopwatches on this play, too. The punter has an average of 2.5 seconds from when the center starts his pass to get rid of the ball, so Jim Ringo's long pass has got to come back there fast as well as with accuracy.

Your two guards, split about a yard from your center, are your principal blockers, and your tackles are a combination of blockers and coverage men. Your two ends rarely have to block and they're mainly coverage-containment men, responsible for the outside against the runback. Two yards back

145

of the ball, and in those gaps between the guards and center, you have two fast halfbacks. We use Elijah Pitts and Herb Adderley. As our fullback we use Bubba Forester. He's the safety valve stationed in front of the kicker to pick up the man somebody else was supposed to get. Only one man can block a kick, because it must be blocked from straight in front of the punter's foot, and Forester is big and agile and experienced enough to make that selection and then handle the most dangerous man.

"All right!" I say now. "Punt return."

Phil Bengston gives them the new assignments he worked out this morning. He reviews for them quickly the setup of our screen for the outside return to either the right or the left.

"Field goal!" I say. "And everybody remember to make yourself as big as you can. Take as wide a stance as you can and get set."

We watch them assume their positions and then I call them all together in a squad huddle. Once again I must tell them things they have heard over and over, and you run out of new ways to say them.

"Okay," I say. "Let's keep off our feet today. A lot of rest. Bed by eleven. Now this is a big one. Every time you can knock off a contender you're making your job a lot easier. You must do it, and this is a real football team you're going to meet. Everybody in the country is interested in this game. Everybody thinks this is the game of the year. Now let's show them a great Packer team!"

Then they all shout together and slap their hands together and the huddle breaks. Phil and I follow them up the ramp and into the dressing room. To play with confidence a team must feel that everything possible has been done to prepare it fully for the coming game and there is nothing more we can tell them. I hope we have given them that confidence.

"He'll see him this afternoon," Jim Nellen says to me in the coaches' office. He had just been talking on the phone with Gene Brusky about Jimmy Taylor. "If he hasn't got a sore throat he should be all right."

1:10 P.M.

I tee off at Oneida with Jack Koeppler, Frank Cornelison and Jack Adams. This is only the third time I've had a chance

146

to play since we went into training camp on July 15. No one mentions football, and my first drive is right down the middle. But it's no use trying to play this game during the football season. I'm only one over par coming up to the fourth hole, but then I hook one into the woods on the left. On the sixth you have to cross that river with your second shot to get to the green, and I use a wood and put it into the water and take the pitching wedge and do the same thing. I finish with an 88, which is six strokes off my game, and when I get home I realize I've left my hat at the club.

6:45 P.M.

Doris and Ockie Krueger have arrived from Milwaukee. Ockie commanded a regiment in Korea during the fighting, was a colonel and Graduate Manager of Athletics at West Point while I was there and now he manages our Milwaukee operation. Doris and Marie are discussing the relative merits of pachysandra versus myrtle as ground cover when Susan comes in. She is wearing a new plaid skirt and Vincent's high school varsity-football sweater.

"How do I look?" she says, turning around for us.

"Has Vincent given you permission to wear that?" Marie asks.

"Nope."

"Well, you'd better not wear it. Go out and get one of your father's old Fordham sweaters."

"His old Fordham sweaters?" Susan says. "Where are they?"

"In the back closet."

When she comes back she has on the white crew-necked sweater with the maroon F. It meant a lot to me once, but now it is so old that the white wool has turned to a cream-yellow.

"Doesn't it look funny?" Susan says.

"You should bleach it," I say.

"You can't bleach old wool," Doris says. "You can never get it white again."

"I don't want to wear it anyway," Susan says.

I call Jimmy Manci. I ask him to reserve a quiet table for us.

"When do you want to come over?" he asks.

"How about a half hour?"

"Can you wait a little longer?" he says. "Your opponents are eating here now."

It's always the other people. You can't even get away from them when you want to eat.

"How long will they be?" I ask.

"How about forty-five minutes?" he says. "They should be gone by then."

"All right."

"What do you mean by a quiet table?" he says.

"Just in a corner somewhere," I say.

7:50 P.M.

Jimmy has given us a corner table but it doesn't help much. I have autographed two menus and the back of somebody's business card, and now I feel another tap on my shoulder and a plump, dark-haired man in his mid-thirties is standing here looking at me.

"Mr. Lombardi?" he says.

"Yes, sir?"

"I'm from Saginaw, Michigan," he says.

"Very good," I say, because he has been waiting for me to say something.

"I'm here to see you get beat," he says.

What am I supposed to say now? I just look at him, and then at the others at our table.

"But I think you've got a good team," he says.

"Thank you."

"Do you think you'll win?" he says.

Here we go again. I should say no. I should say no, that we're just going out for the exercise and expect to be beaten.

"We're going to try," I say, and this is ridiculous.

"How's the weather going to be tomorrow?" he says now.

"I don't know."

"It'll be a better game if it doesn't rain," he says, still hanging on.

"That's right."

"Well," he says, "may the better team win."

"That's right," I say again.

"Well," he says, sticking out his hand. "Good night."

"Good night," I say, shaking his hand.

"Did you ever?" Doris Krueger says, after he has left. "Did you ever hear anything like that in your life?"

"Yes," I say.

The others have gone to bed, but there is no point in my trying to sleep, so I'm watching an old movie on television. Douglas Fairbanks, Jr., is the African white hunter who has hired out to the German baron with the beautiful young wife—and the trouble with me is that my ego just can't accept a loss. I suppose that if I were more perfectly adjusted I could toss off defeat but my name is on this ball club. Thirty-six men publicly reflect me and reflect on me, and it's a matter of my pride.

The German baron wounds a leopard but refuses to track him into the bush. A native bearer is killed by the animal because of the baron's cowardice—and I wonder sometimes if perhaps I transmit to my team the anxiety I feel going into a game. Up to this season no team I have ever been associated with has ever beaten the Colts in Baltimore. Twice the Giants lost to them there and three times they've beaten us there. Does my team absorb a sense of insecurity from me? Detroit has that Night Train Lane and there is no defensive back I respect more. For a couple of seasons Boyd Dowler couldn't do a thing against Lane, and I wondered then if unwittingly I was conveying what I felt to Boyd.

Douglas Fairbanks, Jr., flies his own two-seater plane. One afternoon he and the baroness go out together to scout for game from the air—and what somebody said about a nervous mother making a nervous child may apply to coaching. I know that the first time we played in New York I wanted to win so much I could taste it. If somebody had dropped a pin in the dressing room before the game they would have exploded, and I hadn't been aware that I was transmitting this. How is it transmitted? I don't know, but I know that the Giants beat us 20 to 3.

When Douglas Fairbanks, Jr., and the baroness are forced down by a thunderstorm they are unable to take off again until the next morning. Back in camp there is a violent scene involving the two of them and the baron—and if we don't beat these other people tomorrow it's going to be a tough season. They were breathing on our necks most of last year, and if we don't take them tomorrow they'll be top dogs and we'll have no picnic trying to catch them.

That afternoon the baron wounds a lion and Douglas Fairbanks, Jr., goes into the bush after him. He kills the lion but his arm is torn—and while I've been telling them all week that this is the toughest ball club they're going to have to meet this year I hope I've still been building confidence and not insecurity. How can I be sure?

The way it all comes out is that the baroness realizes that she is really in love with Douglas Fairbanks, Jr. She had married the baron only for his money, and the baron, who must be very well adjusted, accepts the defeat.

SUNDAY

9:25 A.M.

Marie and Susan and I are back from eight o'clock Mass at St. Matthew's, and Ockie Kreuger has made breakfast. We are sitting at the table in the dinette, finishing our coffee, when it finally enters my consciousness that someone has been talking to me.

"Excuse me," I say, looking at Doris Krueger and then Marie. "Did you say something?"

"Are you with us or not?" Marie says.

"I beg your pardon?"

"Come on," Marie says. "Your country needs you. Smile."

Smile? How can I smile? I have been sitting here not knowing whether I'll have Jimmy Taylor, not knowing whether Paul Hornung's leg will be all right and wondering about Tom Moore's shoulder. I have been sitting here thinking of those two big tackles and that middle linebacker and that 81 back there at left defensive halfback.

Smile?

"That's better," Marie says. "Thank you."

"That's better?" Doris says. "Did you ever see such a sick smile?"

We have got to move those tackles and that 56 backing them up, I am thinking as I get up from the table. We may catch them guessing wrong now and then, but if we beat them it will be because we move them or contain them, and do it over and over again. We are going to have to take it right to them, as we did in that second game with them last year, and we beat them then.

I walk into the living room and Ockie follows me. I look out the window. The sky is still low and the air is loaded

150

with moisture that has condensed into droplets on the shrubs and the lawn.

"At least it's good for the grass," I say, resolving to be a sociable host.

"The lawn is beautiful," Ockie says. "How often do they feed it?"

"I don't know," I say. "Three or four times a year."

"Periodic feeding," Ockie says. "It's much better than one heavy feeding in the spring."

"That blue spruce out there is a new one," I say, still trying, "but it looks sick to me."

"Those junipers are nice," Ockie says, trying, too. "A couple of them need some pruning, and if they do it just before Christmas, Marie can use the cuttings for decorations around the house."

"Christmas?" I say. "All our Christmases are hectic. In 1960 we didn't even have one. We just took off for the play-off game in Philadelphia and we didn't even have a tree. Last year was hectic, too."

"You can't have everything, coach," Ockie says. "I'd better shave now."

"I've got to leave soon anyway," I say. "I might as well get out there and see what happens."

"I'll see you later," Ockie says, "and good luck."

10:15 A.M.

As I drive across the bridge at De Pere the first drops of rain hit the windshield. This is not going to help us a bit, but it's not going to help them, either. When I turn into the divided highway there is a bus ahead of me. In the back seat two small boys are wrestling and I see one head emerge and an arm encircle it and the head disappears. Then the other head comes up and another arm rises and curves around it and the second head disappears.

If we're going to take it right to them, I'm thinking, let's do it on the first play. The first time we get that ball let's go right to their strength, and if that's where we're going our Brown Right-73 might be the one to open with at that. I like it, come to think of it, because there's no doubt about that middle linebacker of theirs being a great one and the sooner we go to work on him the better. What I like about it now is that it will give us at least two people on the middle linebacker, and while I don't think we're going to discourage him we should, if Jim Ringo and Ron Kramer both get good shots at him, force him to be at least a little concerned about where those blockers are coming from. And that could be a help.

As I turn off Oneida Avenue and into the parking area one of the attendants in a yellow cap waves to me. Except for a half dozen cars parked up by the entrance to the dressing rooms the area is empty, and when I walk inside it is ten-twenty-five and only Hank Jordan is there, getting out of his jacket in front of his dressing stall.

"Morning, coach," he says, smiling. "Nervous?"

"No," I say. "Are you?"

"Yes, sir," he says.

I'm telling the truth, and he is, too. The difference is that by now I have done all my planning and almost all my scheming, and he must still play his game. Also, over all the years that I have on him, I have learned to control it, and it won't hit me until that kickoff.

"How do you feel otherwise?" I say.

"Fine, thanks," he says.

I look around the room at the stalls, each with the name card and Johnny Proski's grounds crew is rolling the tarpaulins off the pads above it, the gold pants hanging inside on the right, the green jerseys and blue warm-up sweaters on hangers on the left, the floor of each stall covered with six or eight or ten pairs of football shoes at $23.50 a pair. I walk through the equipment room and Dad Braisher has his air hose out and is inflating the footballs to 13 pounds. I open the door to the visitors' dressing room and wave to their equipment manager, who is the only one in there. Over these stalls the helmets are silver and, hanging within the stalls, the pants are silver and the jerseys white.

I walk outside. Two men are approaching the door, each carrying a sack of ice for the trainers. Then I walk to the ramp and look down at the field. The rain has stopped, at least momentarily, and Johnny Proski's grounds crew is rolling the tarpaulins off the field, green along the sides but brown in the middle from abuse.

"It looks like we may have a little mud battle," Phil Bengston says, walking up to me.

"I'm afraid so," I say. And I'm thinking that after it is over, win or lose, somebody from the press will inevitably ask me whether I think it helped or hurt us.

152

"One thing we know," Phil says. "It evens up any game."

Then Phil goes into the dressing room and I walk under the stands. The refreshment people are setting up, and here and there fans, in rain gear, are coming through the turnstiles even at this early hour. Someone has put a polka on the p.a. system and this cavern is filled with it as I walk into the main ticket office to settle for the tickets I have sold.

"No, I'm sorry," one of our ticket men is saying to someone outside the wicket. "We've been sold out for months, and nobody has turned any in."

When I walk back the odor of boiling hot dogs and grilled hamburgers is in the air, complementing the noise of another polka. In our dressing room Earl Gros and Gary Barnes are undressing and in the trainer's room Ed Blaine and Ron Gassert, our two other first-year men, are standing on the tables and having their left knees taped by Bud Jorgensen and Dominic Gentile.

I pour some citrocarbonate into a paper cup and add water and drink it. Back in the dressing room the veterans are coming in now—Forrest Gregg and Dave Hanner and Jim Ringo—and Hank Gremminger is getting out of his street clothes in front of his stall.

"You gonna grab about three today?" Henry Jordan is saying to him.

"I don't know," Gremminger, the worrier, says. "I've sweated through two T-shirts already."

"Is that a good sign?" Jordan says.

"Sure," Gremminger says. "I had breakfast and I was sweating so much I had to change, and now this one's soaked. That's the way I like to be, though."

"How about you?" Ringo says to Hanner. "You give the doctor another workout?"

"That's right," Hanner answers.

"What's the matter with you?" I ask Hanner.

"I felt hot and cold yesterday," he says.

"Did you go to the doctor?"

"Yes, sir. Then last night I went to bed at eight. I woke up at ten sweatin' like anything, but I feel better today."

I hope, I'm thinking. I hope you do, and I hope Jimmy Taylor walks in saying he feels better, too.

"How's Jim?" Ringo says. "Anybody know?"

"He says he had 101," Hanner says, "but he says he's gonna play."

Ron Kostelnik comes in, and he's wearing a new black

153

fedora. Ringo has stripped by now and he takes the hat and puts it on.

"How do I look?" he asks.

"Like a hog head," Gregg says.

"I know why Jordan would buy one of these," Ringo says to Kostelnik. "He'd buy anything to cover that bald head, but I don't understand you."

"I'm gonna grow hair yet," Jordan says. "The next thing I'm gonna try is sheep dip."

Well, they're loose enough, I'm thinking, walking into the coaches' room. They've been too loose the last couple of days, but they'll be all right. It's much better than having them sitting around here like they're waiting for a time-bomb to explode. They'll come up for this one.

Red Cochran is holding his dark blue Packer blazer in his left hand and, with his right hand wrapped in white tape, the adhesive side out, he is brushing lint off it. Phil Bergston is talking to Norb Hecker about yesterday's U.C.L.A. upset of Ohio State, and Bill Austin is on the phone checking with the airport about the weather.

"It could be off and on," he says when he hangs up. "Light rains all afternoon. The wind is East Northeast, 10 to 12 knots. That's about 12 to 15 miles an hour. That's surface winds, and they're different up higher."

"That's not the way the flags are blowing out there," Phil says.

"They're liable to be any way out there," Bill says.

I'm sitting at my desk and still thinking about our Brown Right-73 for our opening play, and I take a yellow lined pad and I diagram it:

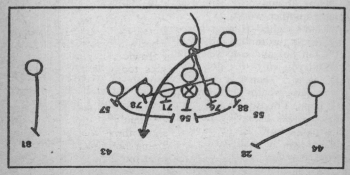

What I still like about that play, looking at it on paper now, is that it really goes to work on that middle linebacker. Jim Ringo sets him up with a drive block for Ron Kramer, who releases from his tight-end spot and comes across and bull-blocks him. Jimmy Taylor fakes up the middle and then takes that big 76 at right tackle. It's a tough block for Jerry Kramer on that 71 at left tackle, but if they give Hornung any daylight and his thigh is all right he should go. Another nice thing about it, too, is that it's a good influence play on their left end. Forrest Gregg pulls across his face, making him think the play is going outside, and when it goes inside you've got that trap on him.

"Bill?" I say.

"Yes?"

"Will you go over with your line our blocking on our 73? We're going to open with it."

"Right," he says.

I'm looking at our Ready List now, in its plastic envelope, the right formations on the one 8 x 11 card, the left formations on the card on the other side. The running plays are listed above the holes where they are designed to go, the passing plays are listed below, and I jot down a half dozen plays, any of which could be logical calls in our first sequence, depending on the result of our 73 and the reaction to it and to whatever we follow with it.

"Red?" I say.

"Here," Cochran answers.

"I want you people upstairs to keep your eyes open about how quick that safety man comes up on the strong side. I want to know if they're trying to keep Ron Kramer from releasing inside."

Red and Tom Fears will be up in the press box spotting for our offensive team and connected by phone with Johnny Roach on our sideline. Norb Hecker will be up there for the defensive team, phoning down to Howie Williams.

"But you won't get any pictures today in this weather," Red says.

"I know."

In good weather Red takes Polaroid shots of anything unusual, or otherwise troublesome, that the opponent is doing defensively. We can then show these to our offensive team right on the sideline or during halftime.

"And Bill," I say, "let's not forget our 5-2 cards."

"Right," he says.

Each week, because you can't practice everything for every game, you take a number of calculated risks. This week we gambled that, although a couple of years ago the other people used a 5-2 defense against us, they would not use it today, so we spent no time devising and practicing an offense against it. We've seen it and drilled for it before, though, and so if we get it thrown at us today there should be no panic. We'll bring out those 5-2 cards on the sideline and show our offense the charts and the list of plays. In fact, a few years ago the Bears used to throw so many defenses at us that we couldn't possibly prepare fully for all of it and for every Bear game we were carrying to the sideline one of those big expansion envelopes filled with charts and play lists.

"How's Jimmy Taylor?" I say to Gene Brusky as I see him walk in.

"He had 101 last night," Gene says. "At midnight I took him off the medication. His temperature is normal this morning."

"Very good."

"I told him," Gene says, "that he's got to play a great game to make me look like a good doctor."

"—and I was thinking of it last night," Hank Gremminger, in his football pants and green jersey, is saying to Phil Bengston.

"The goal line?" Phil says, and he goes to the blackboard. He draws one of the other people's pet goal-line pass plays. Gremminger looks at it, thanks him and leaves.

"They know it just as well as we do," Phil says, "but they want to go over it and over it. They've got to have it letter-perfect, and confidence is the big thing."

Then I walk out to find Jimmy Taylor. It is quiet in the big room now. Most of them have finished dressing and are sitting in front of their stalls. If they are talking at all it is in low voices. Ron Kramer and Dan Currie are lying on their backs in front of their stalls, each with a towel under his head on the floor of his stall, legs up on a chair, eyes closed.

"Jim?" I say to Taylor. "How do you feel?"

He is pulling his jersey on over his head. When he turns I can see that his eyes are glossy and heavy, but whether that's from the fever or the medication I don't know.

"I'm all right now," he says.

"The fever gone?"

"Yeah," he says, "but I had 101."

"The doctor says you're going to be all right."

"I hope so," he says.

And I hope so, too. He is one of those performers who has to be emotionally up and I'm hoping not only that the fever hasn't drained him physically but also that it hasn't defeated him psychologically.

"I'm not even sure," Max McGee is saying, "that I should have gotten dressed. Does anybody know if the other people have shown up?"

"Jim? Bubba?" I say, and I get Ringo and Forester, our two captains, together. "If you win the toss, receive. If we have to kick off, take the north goal."

They both nod yes.

"And, Jim," I say, "if they're doing anything different out there today get a good look at it so we can discuss it when you come out."

"Yes, sir."

"Jesse," I say to Whittenton, walking by him. "How are you?"

"Fine, coach."

I don't have to remind him. He remembers as well as I do that broken-pattern play a year ago when he relaxed on that split end, that 89, and that 89 started up again and Jesse slipped and they hit right over him. I don't have to remind him, but it's in my mind.

"Willie," I say to Willie Davis, who is sitting there silent and, I know, worrying about his own performance, "you're going to have a great day."

"I hope so, coach," he says. "I'll try."

In the coaches' room Red Cochran is copying the Ready-List into a pocket notebook. I change into slacks and pull on a pair of white woolen socks and the ripple-soled coaching shoes.

"All right," I say, "I want the quarterbacks in here."

"Bart! Johnny Roach!" Red Cochran calls as the others leave the room.

When Starr and Roach come in they sit down at the table, with Red Cochran standing behind them, and I sit down across from them. There are no notebooks now, because what they have in those notebooks and playbooks isn't going to help them, or us, if it isn't in their heads. By this time I have cut the number of our running plays down to a dozen and our passes to a half dozen, and I recite them.

"Generally," I say, "your sweeps should be to your left.

157

As far as your pitchout is concerned, I'd use 48 to the left side. When you're going for short yardage you know you can expect the 6-1, so you use those short-yardage and goal-line plays we've been working on.

"Versus the 6-1 these are all right formations," I say, and I enumerate several of them. "Now your 39-Toss can be run provided they don't bring that safety up outside. Against the Frisco your 34-X and 24 should be good. If they go to the Frisco Strong, just turn it around."

As I look at them they are intent and nodding. "Now for our first play let's try the 73. That's whether they're in the 6-1 or 4-3 or whatever they do. Okay?"

"Yes, sir," Starr says.

"On the goal line," Roach says, "had we better run 66 or 67?"

"Well," I say, "that 66, because it's to the left, would be the choice, except we run 67 better. Therefore I think that would depend upon what kind of success you're having. All right?"

"Yes, sir," Roach says.

"Yes, sir," Starr says.

As they get up and leave I look at my watch and it is 12:01 P.M. I follow them to the door of the dressing room.

"All right!" I shout. "Out in fifteen minutes! Let's start getting this dressing room cleared!"

"Players only!" Norb Hecker is shouting, as there are several members of the press and radio who have stopped in. "Players only!"

I sit down at my desk and make a few notes on a small pad. All week I have been talking to them about the importance of this game and so it is difficult on Sunday to think of still another way of saying it. After we come back from our warm-up, though, and it comes up at twelve-fifty-five, I have got to send them out with some kind of a blast-off.

"I just took a look out there," Tom Fears is saying, "and it's starting to rain again."

"It'll rain on them, too," Red Cochran says.

I look at my watch and it is twelve-thirteen and I put on my topcoat and transparent raincoat over it. I walk to the door of the dressing room and look at them, at the rectangle of them sitting in front of their dressing stalls. All of them are now in uniform and wearing olive-green rain jackets and dark blue knitted skull caps. All of them are waiting.

"All right!" I say. "When we get out there let's have a good

158

workout. You ends and backs, take a good look to see where it's soft. Are we all set?"

"Yes!" they holler, all standing up.

"Then let's go!"

"Let's go!" they shout, and they clap their hands in unison and start filing out. Their cleats make the sound of hailstones hitting the concrete and, as I follow them out and look up, the rain, still light and hesitant, hits my face.

"Hey, Paul! . . . Jimmy! . . . C'mon, Max!" the crowd, packed on either side of the walkway to the ramp, is shouting. "Jim Ringo! . . . Hey, Fuzzy! . . . Ray Nitschke! . . . Bart! Hey, Bart! . . . Good luck, Ron! . . . Willie! Good luck, Vince!"

With Phil and Bill and Dick Voris I follow them down the ramp and out onto the field. The stands are about two-thirds full and as we appear a roar floods down from them. We head for the far end zone and I stop and pick a couple of tufts of grass and stand there and throw one up and then the other. Right now the wind is happily not too strong and out of the northeast; so if we lose the toss and have to kick off we will stay with that choice of north goal.

In that far end zone Ringo and Forester are leading them in calisthenics. Behind me I again hear the roar from the stands and I turn and see the other team, in their silver and white uniforms, coming out, down the ramp and out onto the field.

We take the west half of the field now. Boyd Dowler and Max McGee are kicking to our punt-receivers and the coverage men are running down under the kicks. The receivers then throw to the offensive ends and backs, who run the balls back to the kickers.

"C'mon, Boyd" I'm shouting to Dowler. "Get your foot into it!"

Johnny Symank drops a kick. Jimmy Taylor drops a pass. What kind of a day is this going to be?

"C'mon! C'mon!" I say. "Let's catch that ball!"

At the 38-yard line, with Bart Starr holding, Paul Hornung and Jerry Kramer are practicing field goals. I stand behind them and watch for a while, then I turn and search the other side of the field until I find him, that other coach, my counterpart, and I walk over to him.

"How are you?" I say, and we shake hands.

"Fine," he says. "You?"

"All right," I say. "We drew a rotten day."

"We can't do anything about that."

"I'm sorry about the condition of the field, though," I say. "We've had rain most of the week, and they had a high school game here Friday night."

"I understand," he says.

"Well," I say, because he wants no more of this talk than I do. "Good luck, and I'll see you."

"Thanks," he says. "The same to you."

As I turn I see that the referee is bringing over No. 56, that great middle linebacker of theirs. All week, day and night, he had been invading my thoughts, and I have put in that opener just for his benefit. Now we shake hands. Ringo and Forester have joined us. Then I leave, and I'm aware that the light rain seems to have stopped.

On our side Starr and Johnny Roach are alternating, throwing to our pass-receivers and defensive backs. I watch for a while, then turn as Ringo and Forester come back.

"We won the toss," Ringo says. "We receive and they took the north goal."

"Good," I say. Now I'm hoping that we can make something of it. If we can go all the way from that first kickoff it could make the difference in a game like this one figures to be.

I walked down to where Bill Austin and Phil Bengston have the offensive and defensive lines facing one another. They are reviewing assignments. It is now twelve-forty-five. We have been out a half hour, so I send them in, follow them up the ramp and into the dressing room.

They have tried the ground now and some of our backs and receivers are changing from the shorter to the longer cleats. Some of our defensive linemen resist the extra taping on their wrists. They hold off until the last minute, and they are having it done now. When they are all seated in front of their stalls, facing the center of the room, the other coaches and I leave them and go into our room and shut the door.

It is ten minutes to game time, and these three minutes that will follow, with just the squad members alone in the dressing room, is something I started when I first came here in 1959. I was reaching for anything then, any method or device, that would give them a feeling of oneness, of dependence upon one another and of strength to be derived from their unity, so I told the captains that before each game this period would belong solely to the players.

I do not know what is said in that room. I know that Ringo or Forester, or perhaps both, speak, and that if someone else wants to say something he does. I know that at the end—and this is completely their thought and desire—they all join in the Lord's Prayer. Then someone knocks on our door and the other coaches and I walk back into the room.

They are still sitting on those chairs. Some of them are relacing their shoes, some are readjusting their shoulder pads and here and there one is talking to another in a low voice. Now I have seven minutes and I walk among them.

"Willie," I say to Willie Wood, "let's see you grab a couple today."

"I'll be tryin'," Willie says.

"Paul," I say to Hornung, "it's going to take a top effort today."

"I know," he says.

"Bart, let's just relax and have a good ball game."

"Yes, sir," Starr says.

"And, Jerry," I say to Jerry Kramer, "remember to set to the inside, because your guy likes the inside rush."

"I know," he says. "I remember."

"And, Max," I say, "you've always had a good game against this club. You can do it again today."

"I'll try, coach."

"And remember," I say, "when you see that linebacker blitzing, cut off your route sooner."

"Right, coach."

I walk to the center of the room, and I'm running through my mind those notes I made on that small pad. I start out by going over, for the offense, the automatics we're going to use, the plays our quarterback will call on the line when he sees that the defensive alignment will negate what he called in the huddle, and I stress our 36 and 50.

"Now, we're going to receive," I say then, "and we've got the south goal. Remember that this club puts their speediest men as third men out from each side and they must be blocked. They must be blocked, so let's take them out of there. Let's impress them, all of them, right on that kickoff.

"I don't have to tell you," I say, "about the importance of this ball game. You know as well as I do that you're meeting today the top contender, and that no one can win it now but you. For two years these people have been on our necks, but if you beat them today you'll be making your own job easier for the rest of this year. For you to do it, though, is going to require a top effort. You know the spirit with which this other club is coming in here. You know that they think they can beat you, that they've said they will. That's why I say it's going to take a top effort.

"And now," I say, "I want you, all of you, to know this. Regardless of what happens today this is a team of which I am proud. Regardless of the outcome today I'll still be proud of you. To win, though, you're going to have to run harder and tackle harder and block harder. It's going to take a great team effort, so let's have it! Let's go!"

"Let's go!" they shout, standing, and they bring their hands together in unison again. "Let's go! Go!"

There is the roar of the crowd again, the faces and bodies bordering the walkway. There is the jam-up going down the ramp, and we stand, waiting amid the shouts, for the p.a. announcer to introduce the offensive team.

"At center," he says, the sound of his voice filling the air, and Jim Ringo runs out onto the field through the V formed by the cheerleaders and the Green Bay Lumberjacks' band, "No. 51—Jim Ringo! At right guard, No. 64—Jerry Kramer! At left guard, No. 63—Fuzzy Thurston! At right tackle . . ."

We follow the rest of the squad out, Bill Austin, Phil Bengtson, Dick Voris and I. Now the names in the air are those of the other club's starting team, and then Ringo and Forester are walking out to the center of the field for the reenactment of the coin-tossing. When they come back the roar from the stands is beating down in waves around us and I am in the middle, crouching, with the squad pressing in around me.

"So we all know what this means," I am saying. "We all know what it means. We know we've got to go out there and hustle. We know we've got to go out there and hit. So let's do it. Let's take it to them. Let's go!"

They break then, with their exclamations, and our kickoff-receiving team runs out to my right. From the other sideline the other team is peeling out of its huddle. And now that nervousness which I have forestalled, which I have learned to control up to a point, starts to come.

And don't let's drop this kickoff, I'm thinking. This is it now, and please let's not fumble this. Please let's not give them anything they don't deserve.

I watch the referee's arm come down and then I hear the whistle, and to my left that line of white shirts and silver pants and helmets moves forward and I see that ball rise. Then I see our team start to form, and I glance up and see the ball again, it is high and going deep. In our end zone Tom

162

Moore is moving back for it, and I hope he doesn't run it out. He catches it and touches it down.

So that's all right, I'm thinking, pacing while they bring the ball out to the 20 and our personnel changes. That's fine, and now for our Brown Right-73, and let's take it right to them and, most of all, let's get two good shots at that middle linebacker. Just let's do that.

I watch us come out of the huddle and, when our line takes its stance, I can see we're in Brown Right with Jimmy Taylor lined up behind Bart Starr and Hornung to the left. I'm watching that middle linebacker now and I can't hear Starr because of the crowd's roar. I see us start and Starr pivot and that middle linebacker, that 56, held by Taylor's fake into the middle. Now I see Ringo, coming out of there, driving that middle linebacker and then big Ron Kramer hits him high and from somewhere someone else—it's 78, Norm Masters—gets a piece of him and that middle linebacker goes back a good 5 yards, and now he's on his back.

As I look for Hornung and the ball it's all over. They have started to unpile and it appears to be on the 24-yard line. We picked up only 4 yards and we should have got more, but I'll settle for what we got and the way we handled that 56.

"Who made the play?" I say. "Who made the tackle?"

"It was 71," Phil Bengtson says.

Jerry Kramer's man, I'm thinking. I knew it was a tough block and I said so, and that's all right.

"4-4!" Bill Austin is shouting, calling the other team's defense.

Once more I can't hear Starr's count, but I can tell from the length of it that he's going to an automatic, and audible check-off. We are in Blue Left Inside, with Ron Kramer lined up to the left in slot position, and this should be our 36. If it is it involves that Do-Dad—with Ringo, Thurston and Skoronski, and with Ron taking that end in the direction he wants to go and Taylor running to daylight either outside or inside that end.

He runs inside now as Ron takes that end out and Thurston puts a great block on that big left tackle, that 76. He drives him back and to the inside, but in addition to being big, that 76 is a real football player. Taylor is through the hole, but 76 recovers and hauls Jimmy down after an 8-yard gain.

"How to drive, Jimmy!" someone is hollering. "First down! First down!"

"Frisco!" Bill Austin is shouting. "Frisco!"

It's another audible, and either our Red Right-50 or our 51 would be a good call. We are in Red Right and it is our 50 and I can hear those shoulder pads pop and Hornung picks up 7 yards right up the middle before that 71 frees himself from Jerry Kramer's block and makes the tackle.

Now we are in Blue Left Inside. If it's our 61 it is also designed to go up the middle, but that 71 wants to come inside, as we told Jerry he likes to do, so Jerry takes him where he wants to go and Taylor runs it to the daylight outside of him and carries 6 yards and it's another first down.

This is the way to play this game, I'm thinking, aware now of the roar from the stands and that it has started to rain again. We're driving off the ball and blocking the stuffing out of them and let's keep it going. Let's go all the way while we've got them rocking on their heels.

We are in our Red Right again. Starr is dropping back now, to pass for the first time, and it is our Backs Divide, with Taylor going out to the right side and Hornung to the other. Jimmy, though, is picking up that left linebacker, as we told him to do when that man blitzes. I look downfield and Max McGee is wide open but Starr throws to Hornung in the left flat and the ball is off Paul's fingertips.

All right, I think. All right. We told him when they blitz to throw to Paul, but we can change. Let's not lose our momentum.

"Blue! Blue!" I can hear their middle linebacker calling now, and since those three hit him on that first play he has been all eyes. "Blue!"

"4-3!" Bill Austin is hollering.

Starr is dropping back again. It is our 6-pattern, and Taylor swings to the left and McGee goes down the left and gives the right defensive halfback a good fake to the outside and then goes inside. He is out there and Starr throws. Max makes a fine leaping catch and now it is first and 10 and we are down on the other club's 41.

It is right out of those movies we watched this week. Max ran it well against them last year and on Friday I showed it to him on the screen again. Now let's keep this parade moving.

We are in our Red Right and, as we come off the ball, that middle linebacker and their right linebacker blitz. It is our 51 with Taylor, though, and when the middle linebacker

164

blitzes it becomes a trap on him. He gets a hand on Jimmy but Jimmy is by him and then he bounces off somebody else and he is going . . . going . . . and he is down to their 14 before somebody stops him.

That's how sick our Jimmy is, I'm thinking. It was a great effort, and now we're in Blue Right and somebody breaks through and throws Hornung behind the line.

"What was that supposed to be?" I say.

"I think 64," Bill Austin says, "but there's a penalty."

"Who's it on?"

"On them," Phil Bengtson says. "Personal foul."

Halfway to the goal, I'm thinking, and that's a break. That puts it on about the 7, and this is where it gets tough. If we can just keep coming off that ball and blocking in there the way we have been. . . .

"They make it first and 8 to the goal," Phil says.

"Go, Big Green!" someone behind me is hollering.

So let's find that defense now, I'm thinking. They'll be in 6-1, as we guaranteed they'd be inside their 10, and we go into Blue Right with Taylor behind Starr and Hornung to the right. From that, on Wednesday night, we settled on our 64 or our 37.

It's our 37. It's Taylor, driving for that 7 hole off Gregg's outside shoulder, but there's a pile-up. Somebody closed that hole and Jimmy made only a yard.

"What happened?" I say. "Anybody see who it was?"

I know who it was, I'm thinking. It was that left linebacker, and that's Ron Kramer's man. When they're in that 6-1 Ron has to take that left linebacker and it must have been Ron's man.

"It was either the left linebacker or the safety," somebody says.

Now we're in Red Right. In their 6-1, when we go into Red, their middle linebacker will line up to his left, opposite our fullback, and that's where he is now. We told them that, too, and we talked about running away from him with our 28-Weak Side Sweep.

"Weak Side Sweep," Bill Austin says.

It starts to the left and the tackle takes the end. Hornung has to take the right linebacker but that man reads the play and moves to the outside and it is a tough block for Paul. As Taylor tries to cut he loses a step when his left foot slips on the wet turf, and their inside pursuit cuts him off and we lose a yard.

"Lew!" I'm hollering to Carpenter because I want to rest Hornung for a field goal. "Go in for Paul!"

It is third and 8 now, and we are in Blue Right. Starr fakes our 37 to Taylor and rolls out to his right. Ron Kramer is running a corner pattern to his right and Starr spots him deep in the end zone and throws. Ron appears to have his man beaten, but the ball is overthrown. We come 80 yards and miss by an inch.

"All right, Paul!" I say. "Let's go! Field-goal team!"

We should have had 7 points, I'm thinking. We came all this way from our own 20 and we should have had 7. That 37 from the Blue was the play, and I told them they'd see that 6-1. Ron should have recognized that, and let's get 3, at least, now. Let's make ourselves big out there and let's get at least 3.

We get the 3. Hornung puts it right between those posts, but we still should have had 7.

"Way to run, Jim!" Hank Jordan is saying to Taylor. "Keep stingin' 'em boy!"

Hornung kicks off high to them, now, and we're quick getting down there, and their 21 gets back only to the 14-yard line. I turn now and search the bench until I find Ron Kramer and I go over to him.

"What's the matter, Ron?" I say. "On that Blue Right-37 you're supposed to take that linebacker."

"I did," he says, looking up at me, puzzled. "That's what you told us."

Now it dawns on me. It wasn't Ron and it wasn't that middle linebacker. It had to be Hornung and the left safety, that 43, must have been the one who stopped it.

"Hey, Paul!"

"Yes, sir?" he says walking over to the table.

"On Blue Right-37, you're supposed to take the safety. We went over it this week. What's the matter? Can't you . . ."

"I know," he says, nodding. "I blew it."

Great. We should have had 7. Just great, I'm thinking, and I take the phone from Johnny Roach and look up at the press box.

"Red?" I say. "Tom?"

"Tom, Vince," Fears says.

"On that Backs Divide, Max is free, isn't he?"

"That's right. Paul can take that blitzing linebacker."

"That's what I thought," I say, handing the phone back to Roach. "And Paul?"

"Yes, sir."

"On that Backs Divide, take that linebacker if he blitzes."

"Yes, sir."

"Bart? Max?"

"Yes, sir," Starr says, and he is at my side.

"Right," Max says, standing up and walking over.

"On that Backs Divide, if the linebacker blitzes, Paul will take him. Max, as I said, you cut off your route sooner, the way you did, and Bart, Max should be open."

"Yes, sir."

I turn back to the field. We've still got them down there near their 20, and Phil Bengtson, to my left, is signaling our defense. His system is like that of a baseball coach and he signals the overall call, storms and blitzes and pass defense.

"How are we?" I say.

"Third and 2," Phil says.

They try a Fullback Draw and Ray Nitschke spots it and they bring out the chain to measure. It is fourth and 1. The other people are sending in their punting team and I send in our punt-return team.

"Left return," I tell Johnny Symank.

It is just a guess—they always are, these right or left returns—and Willie Wood takes it on our 23. Our wall forms and he cuts to his left and comes wide. He picks up only 7 yards, but if somebody had taken that last man Willie would have been gone.

We run our 79 out of the Brown and we were right, up to a point. As early as Tuesday afternoon we were convinced, as soon as we saw their game of last week, that Ron Kramer could handle that left linebacker, and he does. The play takes too long to materialize, though, when Fuzzy Thurston doesn't make his cut into the hole soon enough and we get too much penetration from Forrest Gregg's man. Hornung doesn't belly his run enough, and they hold him to 4 yards.

They hold Taylor to 1 yard on our 34-Cross, but he picks up 9 and the first down on our Draw 4. Now we're in Red Right and here it comes—that Backs Divide—and they're blitzing again. Hornung takes that linebacker, as I just told him, and Max cuts off his route and he's open. Starr hits him over the middle for 10 yards and another first down.

Beautiful, I'm thinking. That's the way to play this game, and now . . .

"Wait a minute!" Bill Austin says. "Penalty. Offside."

"Who?" I say.

"Us," Bill says. "I don't know who it was."

That's the way to play this game? You scheme and adjust and it works, then an offside costs you 15 yards. It costs you the 10 you make and the penalty. Now we fake our 49 and Ron Kramer comes around from tight right end and it's the reverse. He didn't slip when he made his cut on that practice field in that rain on Wednesday, but now he slips and we lose 4, and we're back on our 35 and it's second and 19.

Well, I'm thinking, maybe it will slow down their pursuit a little anyway. At least the threat of that reverse may slow down that quick pursuit just a little from now on.

Ron Kramer makes a great leaping catch over the middle now and we're third and 8. We go into our Double-Wing for the first time.

"Double-Wing!" their middle linebacker, that 56, is hollering. "Double-Wing!"

So it's no surprise to them, but as Hornung moves into the slot, in a position to go out on a quick pass, it's going to force their weak-side safety, who has been playing the middle zone, to play him. The rest of that defensive secondary will have to be more inside conscious, and they won't be as strong to the outside, either.

It fails, though. After a good outside feint Ron Kramer runs a Zig-In, but it takes him too long to make his break to the inside and by then those two tackles I've been worrying about all week, that 71 and that big 76, overpower Thurston and Jerry Kramer and drop Starr for an 8-yard loss.

Boyd Dowler punts dead on their 21, and when they try a weak-side pitchout we get some excellent pursuit ourselves and Jesse Whittenton comes up and tackles their 45 for no gain. We break up two of their passes, one on which their fullback was open, though, and they kick. Willie Wood comes back 22 yards on a right return and we're in good position on our own 41. We run our 28-Sweep again, and get excellent blocks from Ron Kramer and Thurston and Jerry Kramer, but their pursuit defeats us and we pick up only 4. We're in Brown Right and it's an automatic. It's our 36, with that Do-Dad involving our left guard and left tackle, but Jimmy Taylor is too anxious. He doesn't wait for the hole to open, and I hear the thud of bodies when they hit him and I see the ball pop out, and there's a pile up, and the other people recover.

"Defense!" Phil Bengtson is hollering. "Let's go. Hold them there now!"

We were on our own 45 and in good shape, I'm thinking. Now we give it to them on our 42. Fumbles, fumbles! We've got these people pinned and they still haven't made a first down, but a penalty costs us 15 yards in one drive and a fumble takes us out of another, and now they're on our 42 and it's a gift.

"That's all right, Jimmy," I say to Taylor when he comes off. "Don't let it worry you."

Their quarterback is dropping back into his pocket now, but Willie Davis has his man beaten and he's forcing that quarterback out of the pocket. Somebody else takes a shot at Willie, but he pivots off.

"Pursuit! Pursuit!" Willie is hollering.

But where is it? Willie runs over a third man but that quarterback is circling to his right now and he picks up 13 yards before Bill Quinlan comes across from the other end and drives him out of bounds on our 29 as the quarter ends.

"Isn't that something?" Austin says.

"Miserable," Dick Voris says.

I'm looking for Boyd Dowler. We've got to start throwing to him, and we told him to be careful of that left halfback, that 81, on anything to the inside. But I want to check on it now.

"How's he playing you?" I say to Boyd. "What do you think?"

"Gee, coach," he says. "I think I can beat him on Turn-Ins."

"All right," I say. "Give it a try."

The teams have changed goals and are to my left now. Their quarterback hits his split end for 9 yards and he rolls out of bounds on our 20. Their fullback picks up 3 and a first down on a slant, but when they give it to him again he makes only 2 when Hank Jordan gives his guard an inside move and goes outside to make the tackle. They fake to the fullback and hit the left halfback for 5 yards to the 10. It's third and 3 now, but Bubba Forester cracks through on a blitz and drops their quarterback, before he has a chance to unload, on the 18.

"Bubba! Bubba!" they are hollering behind me now. "Big Green!"

"All right!" Phil Bengtson is shouting. "Let's block this field goal!"

They place the ball down on the 25. I see the pass-back, the two lines collide, the kicker's foot comes forward. The ball starts to rise but there are two green shirts through there, arms up, and the ball is bounding back behind their kicker. There is a scramble for it, as the roar comes out of the stands, and there is another green shirt—71, that's Forester —covering it on our 36-yard line.

"Who blocked it?" somebody is asking. "Jordan?"

"Adderley," somebody else says. "How to go, Herb!"

Phil Bengtson was right. He was absolutely right. He said the other morning at Sneezer's that he had guaranteed Bill and Tom that the defense would block the first field-goal try. He was right, and we should get a lift out of this.

Taylor, in two tries, pi s up a first down, but we lose 3 on a Swing-4 Delay pass to Hornung. On our 61-Quick Trap we catch the two linebackers blitzing up the middle and their tackles going to the outside and Thurston and Ringo pick up the blitzers and Taylor goes for 8. On third and 5 and Backs Divide with Hornung delaying, Dowler runs his R Turn-In, and he does beat that 81 and makes a leaping catch and we're on their 36.

"Holding," Bill Austin says. "On us."

"Who?"

"I don't know."

So instead of being first and 1 on their 36 we're third and 27 on our own 30. Now we're in Red Left and Starr is dropping back. It's supposed to be our Fan Circle, L and R Cross, but when he can find nobody open Starr pulls it down and starts to run to his right. As Jerry Kramer cuts in front of him to block one of those white shirts Starr shifts the ball to the other arm and there's a collision and the ball is loose and their 71 is on it on our 34.

Here we go again, I'm thinking. A holding penalty kills a first down and now we fumble and they're in a great spot. Isn't there any justice?

"C'mon, c'mon, defense!" Phil is shouting. "Let's get that ball back."

Their first pass, intended for the fullback, misses but their left halfback picks up 11 outside our left end when they

170

catch us blitzing Nitschke and Forester, and we have no pursuit. Dan Currie holds their halfback to 2 yards on a dive, and Nitschke almost intercepts on a pass intended for their tight end. It's third and 8 now, and if we can stop this I'll settle for their field goal and be glad to get out of this alive.

I'll willingly settle, and now I watch their quarterback drop back and Willie Davis is in there again. He runs right over his blocker but that quarterback gives Willie the straightarm now and he's around him, running to his right down the far sideline and he's down to the 6.

First and goal on the 6. What kind of a day is this, anyway? We almost intercept. Then we cover their receivers and Willie breaks in there and, on a broken pattern, they've got first and goal on the 6.

They are lining up weak side to the left now and we're in 4-3. They give it to their left halfback again on a belly play and he goes to his left and outside, and they give him good blocking, and he scores. I've got to admit it. It was a fine call and beautiful execution, but don't we deserve better than this? They kick the point. And don't we deserve better than being down 7-3?

Tom Moore takes their kickoff on the 7 and brings it back to the 33. On our 61 out of Blue Left the middle linebacker, that 56, stops Taylor on the 35. Dowler gives a good outside move and then flies, but he trips over that 81's leg and just misses Starr's pass. Taylor makes a leaping catch of a Fan pass, runs away from one man and, when Max McGee throws a block that screens two of those white shirts, Jimmy gets down to their 41. Out of Brown Left we run our 72, the reciprocal of our 73, the first play of the game, but Hornung makes only 4 when we don't get that right linebacker out of there.

Now Earl Gros is in, to rest Taylor, and our Do-Dad doesn't work because someone's not thinking and they throw Gros for a 2-yard loss. We go into our Double-Wing and they're still in a 4-4, which surprises me because I thought the Double-Wing would chase them out of it. McGee runs an L Drag-In, and as Hornung clears the area deep, Max breaks in and Starr hits him, and we've got a first down on their 26.

"Tom Moore!" I say. "Go in for Paul, and run the 79-Option."

"Yes, sir," he says, running out.

I have been waiting for the spot to call it. I have been watching that left halfback, their 81, and that left safety come up real hard, and they won't expect Moore to throw it. They'd expect Hornung to throw it, but they shouldn't expect it of Moore, and I look at the clock. There are less than three minutes remaining in the half, and if we can go all the way now we can go into that dressing room ahead.

We go into Brown Right and I watch. We come off the ball and Moore has it, swinging to his right. Our guards are pulling and it looks good. Their left safety is coming up hard and their left halfback is playing it for the run, too. Dowler's down there, open, heading for the end zone, and Moore slows now and throws. I watch the flight of the ball, and it's no good. It's short. It's underthrown, behind Dowler, and their weak-side safety, racing across, makes a great extended catch and falls into the end zone with it.

We had that one. I mean we should have had it, but that's the gamble. I sent Moore in there cold. Hornung's a better passer, but if I had left him in there I doubt that they would have let Dowler get open like that.

"That's all right, Tom," I say, as Moore comes out, shaking his head. "Forget it."

"I'm sorry," Moore says.

They put the ball down on the 1. We give up a first down but then force them to kick. With less than a half minute left on our own 30 I don't want us gambling here and handing them anything else, so I tell Starr to kill the clock and the half ends.

We should have them at least 14 to 7, I'm thinking, walking acrosss the field and up the ramp—at least that. We're beating ourselves, and you can't make those mistakes against a good ball club like this and survive. Two penalties and two fumbles take us out of two drives and we got exactly one break. We got that penalty to the 8 and then Paul either doesn't recognize the 6-1 or he forgets he's supposed to take the safety on our Blue Right-37 and we blow it. Then Dowler is open in the end zone on the option and Tom underthrows it. But this kind of thinking doesn't mean anything. It isn't going to change that first half, and the fact is, except for those gifts and the score, we've been outplaying them. We've just got to come out and do it again, and without the mistakes.

172

The defense has taken the far end of the dressing room, their chairs grouped in front of the blackboard. The offense is seated facing the other way, and the trainers and clubhouse boys are circulating, the trainers with tape and the clubhouse boys with water and towels.

"Now that quarterback is hurting us, rolling out and running," Phil Bengtson is telling the defense. "We didn't expect this, so we've had you outside linebackers dropping back against the pass, and Willie Davis forcing. Dan?"

"Yes?" Currie says.

"You're going to have to move up and take the run. The same with you, Bubba."

"Right," Forester says.

"And you tackles," Phil says. "We gave you the inside rush because we were worried about the middle. They're not hurting us there, so we'll go to the outside rush. This will also contain the roll-out, and should get you to the passer quicker. Ray Nitschke?"

"Yep?" Nitschke says.

"You're going to have to hustle over there," Phil says, "I mean you're going to have to move over there to take Dan's man, or Bubba's to the other side."

"Right."

I turn and join the offense. Bill Austin is talking with the offensive linemen about cross-blocking against a weak-side overshift, answering questions, and Red Cochran and Tom Fears are with the backs and receivers, going over what the other people's defensive backs have been doing on their coverage.

". . . and when we went into the Blue," Tom is saying, "they shifted their secondary."

"That leaves the weak side open," Red says.

"From the Blue," Max McGee says, "I think I can beat my man deep inside or out."

"All right," I say, "and let's look for Max on that, Bart."

"Yes, sir."

"Boyd?" Red says.

"I think I can get open deep on the 9-Pattern."

"Okay," I say. "And Bart, if they go into the Zone let's use the 39-Toss."

"Yes, sir."

"So let's concentrate on the Brown and the Blue," I say. "You've got that 39-Toss from the Blue, the 37 from the

173

Blue, the 61 from the Blue or the Brown, the 73 from the Brown, the 36 from the Brown. I'm not excluding the Red, but let's concentrate on those."

I walk back to the defense. Norb Hecker is at the blackboard briefing them on our pass defense.

"Now we know he tends to throw in patterns," he is saying. "He likes those slants, down-and-ins, turn-ins, rather than outside. Let's remember this, too. He only threw to his flanker once, so we can figure he's going to go to him more this second half. Let's double him every chance we get, play him inside and outside and . . ."

"Five minutes!"

It is the official, his head in the door.

"All right," I say.

". . . and if they're looking for shorter yardage for a first down," Norb is saying, "we go into our Combo, especially if the right end blocks. If he then releases, Dapper takes him here, in the hook zone, and if the flanker turns in, Hank has him on the inside and Herb to the outside. Clear?"

"How about their pass to the fullback?" I say. "He was open."

"I know," Norb says. "We've covered that."

"All right, then. Let's get ready."

"And it's a wet ball," Norb is telling them. "When we get our hands on it let's bring it right to our bodies."

"All right! All right!"

The defense gets up then and moves to the front of the room. The offense remains seated and I walk around and face them and wait for the room to quiet down.

"All right," I say. "We've made our mistakes, but that's all over. That's out of the way and done with. Let's remember this, though. In spite of those mistakes we're right in this ball game. In spite of the fact that they've made no mistakes we're right on their necks, and they will make mistakes. They're yet to come, but they will come. We'll force them. Our defense knows we can stop them. Our offense knows it can move the ball against them. We know we're the better team, but up to now we've stopped ourselves. We've stopped ourselves, but that's over. Now we go. Let's go out and nail them inside the 20 on the kickoff, hold them and get that ball near midfield. So let's go!"

"Let's go!" they shout, clapping their hands in unison again. Then there is the scraping of chairs and the sound of cleats on the floor, and I'm following them out again

I think they feel they can do it. There was an atmosphere of confidence there, I felt. At least I think I did.

As I cross the field the last of the band members are filing off and I'm aware that it is still raining. It has let up some, though, so maybe it is ending.

"All right, now," I'm saying in our sideline huddle. "We've come back many, many times. Many times! Now we can do it again. Let's go!"

"That's right!" somebody shouts. "Let's go, Big Green!"

And now let's not give them a long runback, I'm thinking as I watch us line up to kick off. Let's not give them anything that will provide them with a psychological lift. That's why I want them nailed down there inside the 20. We can't afford to give this club anything now.

"What happened?" I say after Hornung's first kickoff.

"Green offside," Hank Gremminger says.

Too anxious, I'm thinking. But that's all right. I'd rather have them that way, and I watch Hornung's second kick go through the end zone.

We give them a first down on a roughing penalty but get it back when they're called for holding. We force them to kick and we've got it down to my left on our own 22.

"4-3!" Bill Austin is shouting.

They blitz out of it and right into our 52-Counter and stop Taylor for no gain. We go into Red Left, but Ron Kramer is offside. Out of Blue Left, Starr rolls out to his left but overthrows Ron on the opposite sideline, and now we're third and 15.

"Where's our momentum?" I'm saying. "We've lost it."

"Double-Wing!" their middle linebacker is shouting. "Double-Wing!"

Boyd Dowler makes a diving catch over the middle and we're first and 10 on our 37. Taylor picks up 2, but Starr throws behind Max McGee and Max is screaming about interference. Starr is rolling toward me now. It's our Four-X-Switch and Dowler makes a great leaping catch. With that left halfback, 81, on his back, he rolls over, gets up and drives for 2 more yards.

We've got the first down on their 41. On our Swing Delay Taylor picks up their blitzing weak-side linebacker and Ron Kramer takes the strong-side blitz and McGee beats his man on a Down-and-Out and it's another first down and we're on their 27.

All right, I'm thinking, we've got that momentum back

now. We're in Red Left and that middle linebacker moves to his left with Jimmy Taylor, as we said he would. It is Hornung on our 51, but it is taking a little too long to materialize and that big left tackle, that 76, has 75 pounds on Jim Ringo and finally overpowers him and makes the tackle on the 23.

That's all right. We're still in good shape. Now Hornung is swinging to his right and it's our 49-Option and I look down toward the end zone. This time Ron Kramer is open, but this time it's Hornung who underthrows and the left linebacker, that 57, makes a great leap and intercepts and brings it out to the 39 before we get him.

"Defense!" Phil Bengtson calls, and someone behind me is swearing. "Let's go, defense!"

Paul was too cautious. He was aiming. It's the greatest play in football. I think that option play is the greatest play in football, and we run it as well as or better than anyone else. Now we try it twice and we throw for two interceptions.

"Vince!" Dick Voris says. "Phone."

"Yes?" I say, taking the phone. It's Red Cochran. "What?"

"On our Blue now," Red says, "they're playin' that safety deeper."

"You think our 9-Pass might go?"

"Sure."

"All right," I say, handing the phone back to Johnny Roach. "Bart?"

"Yes, sir?"

"On our Blue that safety man is playing it deeper. You might be able to get that 9-Pass in there."

"Yes, sir.".

They have third and 4 on their own 45. This is a big one —all these third downs are getting to be big ones now— and we've got the blitz on and we make him hurry his throw to his tight end and he misses. They kick and Willie Wood calls for a fair-catch on our 20.

"What was that supposed to be?" I say after they've held Taylor to a yard.

"Red Right-22," Bill Austin says.

Let's block out there, I'm thinking. Every week it comes down to the same thing. When we're not blocking we're not moving that ball. The game is as simple as that.

"Blue Right!" I can hear their middle linebacker hollering now. "Blue Right!"

Starr drops back and we fan right. It's that 9-Pass we just

gave him, and Tom Moore splits two whiteshirts to grab it and we have a first down on our 34.

"Oh, no!" I holler after they've thrown Taylor for a yard loss. "Let's go out there!"

"The outside linebackers blitzed," Phil Bengtson says.

Starr fakes to Taylor and drops back. Max McGee is running a split route between the right halfback and right safety, taking them deep as we told him to do, and Starr throws a quick screen pass to Moore in the left flat. We pick up 8 yards. ✓

"Third and 3," Bill says.

Another big one. Let's not die here now, I'm thinking, and we go into Brown Right. It's our 36 and Taylor runs to daylight outside the halfback's block on the right linebacker and it's going to be close. They bring out the chain and measure. We've made it.

Starr is dropping back again, looking toward Ron Kramer. Max McGee has gone down the left side about 20 yards and, when he makes his cut to the inside, the right halfback, playing him tight to the outside, cuts with him. They are a close pair, bumping, and as the ball reaches them Max is falling. They're both falling, and the ball has bounced off someone's hand and it's still in the air. The right safety is coming in for it now, and he has it. I see one greenshirt go down and then another, and their man is back deep in our territory before Tom Moore knocks him out of bounds.

"Ref! Ref!" I'm hollering. "He was all over him!"

"Interference! Interference!" they are hollering around me.

The referee has called time and Jim Ringo is with him, pointing downfield. Their middle linebacker and a couple of others are protesting, but the ball is coming back. We're getting it, and it means a first down on their 40.

And now let's take it to them, I'm thinking. While they're still upset let's take it to them. It's Jimmy Taylor on our 39-Toss. He gets a great block by Jerry Kramer pulling and by Tom Moore, and he runs away from one man and pivots around another, and we've got a first down on their 30. Max McGee runs a perfect L-Zig-Out and Starr fires it right into his hands and we're on their 12. We run a power play, our 47-Drive, with Hornung back in for Moore, and he picks up 5. We've got a second and 5 on their 7, and we're in great shape.

"Tom!" I say to Moore. "Go back in for Jim. Let's run that 36 from the Blue Left, and let's go all the way."

I watch us go into the Blue Left now, Hornung to fake inside or outside that right end of theirs. This is the one we need. I see those lines charge and the hand-off to Moore, but some white-shirt is in there. Some mud-covered white-shirt is in there and we lose a yard.

"The right end," I say when I see him get up. "What's the matter with our left tackle, whoever it is? Why couldn't he get him out of there?"

It's third and 6 now and Starr is faking our 36 and dropping back. Max McGee is running the L-V-Out and has his man beaten but he runs out of field and it goes out of the end zone.

"Field goal!" I say. "Let's go!"

There wasn't enough room for Max's pattern, I'm thinking. We were on the left hash-mark. If we'd been on the right hash-mark or even in the middle it would have been a perfect call, and even if Paul makes this now we're still in a hole, and this period must be about over.

Paul makes it as the quarter ends. We're still down 7-6, though. They're a tough ball club, especially inside their own 10. We knew that, but I thought we could handle that right end on our 36.

That leaves us one quarter to do it or not.

Hornung's kick is 5 yards into the end zone but their receiver finds daylight and he is all the way out to the 34 before a great ankle tackle by Willie Wood drops him. Their fullback picks up 3 yards, Bubba Forester almost intercepts one and on third down, Willie Davis and Dave Hanner throw their quarterback for a 7-yard loss. They kick and we have it on our own 22.

Starr passes to Dowler on a Quick Turn-Out for 5. We're in Red Left, but Hornung makes only 2.

"A blown play," I say. "Whatever it was, wake up out there!"

It's third and 3 now, and this one we really need. We're in Brown Right and when those lines charge they're playing a 6-1. It's our 67, only good against the 6-1, but the right call. There's the hole, but something happens and Hornung gets only a yard.

"He tripped!" somebody says.

"If I don't trip over a leg," Hornung says, shaking his head as he comes out. "I go 20 yards. I go 20 yards at least."

178

Dowler punts. It is high but not deep, and we are down there under it. It is coming down on about their 30-yard line, and at the last moment their receiver starts to raise his arm in what may be a signal for a fair-catch just before he catches the ball, and in that same instant Elijah Pitts, about to tackle him, bumps him.

"No! No!" Bill Austin is screaming as the referee signals interference on the catch. "No! No!"

"No!" I'm hollering at the referee. "No signal! He didn't give a clear signal!"

The referee steps off the 15 yards, and now the ball is on their 46. We get a great rush out of Hank Jordan and Bill Quinlan and their quarterback has to throw the ball away. He hits their flanker on the next one, over the middle, for 13 yards, and they're on our 41. He tries a quarterback draw, but both Jordan and Dave Hanner hit him and he picks up only 3. He goes for the long one to his split end, but Herb Adderley is on him in the end zone. It's third and 7, and he hits his flanker on a Fan Right, but they get only 4 yards, and here comes their other quarterback to hold for the field-goal attempt.

I look at the clock. There are nine minutes remaining. It is too much to expect us to block two in a row, but if they get this one it will take a touchdown to beat them, and we've got only nine minutes.

"Watch the fake!" Phil Bengston is hollering. "Don't be offside!"

Again I watch the pass-back. The lines collide. I watch the kicker take his steps and the ball rise. It's going . . . going . . . deep enough, but it's wide to the left.

"All right!" I say. "Let's block out there now, offense. That's the break we wanted."

We have the ball on our 20 and we go into our Double-Wing. They blitz strong and weak and Starr throws to Max on a Quick Turn-Out for a first down on our 30. We're in Blue Right but on our 9-Pattern, Starr's pass is just off Dowler's fingertips.

"Big play," I say, pacing. "That was a big one right there."

They're all big ones now. Starr hits Ron Kramer on a perfect Fan Right R Turn-In for 15 yards on our 45. The next call is a great one. They're in a 4-3 Zone and Starr calls our Swing Pass Inside Delay. Ron Kramer takes the left linebacker wide. Taylor takes the middle linebacker to the left. The right linebacker plays McGee deep. The right halfback plays him underneath. The right safety goes deep in the hole. Dowler takes his left halfback and the left safety deep and Starr finds Hornung all alone over the middle on a delay for 13 yards and we're on their 42.

"Beautiful!" Phil is saying. "How to go, Green!"

They're blitzing again, but Taylor picks up the man on his side and Ron Kramer takes the left linebacker. The protection is perfect and downfield to my left McGee has his man beaten deep. Starr's pass is short, though, wobbling, and McGee can't get back for it.

"Tom!" I call, looking for Moore. "Go in for Paul. Let's go with our Quick Screen."

We make only 2 yards on it as both linebackers get him. They defense our Fan Pass Left perfectly and stop Taylor for no gain. Now we're fourth and 8 on their 40, and with less than four minutes left I'll settle for a field goal and a 2-point lead. I don't like it, but I'll have to settle for it.

"Field goal! Let's go!"

Hornung's kick is not an end-over-end but a spiral. It squirts off to the right, short, and their 25 runs it back from the 5 to their 22.

"We're standing around and looking at the goalposts!" I'm shouting at them now as they come back. "They might have run it back for a TD!"

"Let's get that ball, defense!" Phil is shouting.

That's our only chance now. We've got to hold them down there and go for that ball. If we don't force a fumble we've got to force them to kick. I look at the clock again and there are less than four minutes remaining.

Their left halfback picks up 5 yards before Ray Nitschke nails him. On a draw Quinlan and Hanner throw him for a 2-yard loss, but on a pass to the tight end in the right flat they pick up the first down on their 34.

"C'mon, Big Green!" they are hollering around me now. "Get that ball!"

They try a Sweep Left but they don't get Bill Quinlan out of there and he holds their halfback to 1 yard. Now their quarterback is rolling to his right, toward me, but with Dan Currie playing it for the run as Phil told him and with the receivers covered we force him to throw it away, over our sideline.

"Big one now, Big Green!" someone behind me is shouting. "Big one!"

It's big all right. It's third and 9 on their 35, and if we don't give them this one . . .

Their quarterback is dropping back again. Their split end has squared out, running toward our sideline, not more than 5 yards to my right, and he makes a diving, sprawling catch, an almost impossible catch as he hits the ground.

"He trapped it!" they're hollering around me now. "He trapped it, ref!"

I wish he had, but he didn't. He made a beautiful catch, his right hand between the ball and the ground, and it was right here in front of me. I can't kick on this one, and they've got a first down on their 47.

"Two minutes, Vince," Bill Austin says. "Vince?"

I look up and see the referee signaling to me, two fingers of his right hand extended. I acknowledge him, and watch them come up to the line. Their fullback makes 3 yards on a slant before Currie stops him, and we call a time-out to stop the clock.

They try a weak-side sweep toward the other side, but Nitschke and Whittenton, coming up fast, throw the halfback for a yard loss. Now it's third and 8 on their 49 and we call another time-out. There is 1:46 left, so if we can hold them here we should get their kick, at the very worst, on our 20 with about a minute and a half left.

"Bart?" I say, turning to Starr. "No huddles now. Try to go with that crossing pattern, and get ready for no huddles."

"Yes, sir."

Bubba Forester has come over to the sideline. Phil Bengtson is talking to him on our 43-yard line.

"Let's remember this is the line they've got to cross," he's saying. "They need 8 yards, so let's play them for the 9-yard pass. Let's go, now!"

"Right," Bubba says, nodding.

I watch him run back out. I watch the other people come out of their huddle and go into Red Right, the flanker to the right and the tight end split about 3 yards. This is our last chance now. If we don't stop this one we'll never get that ball back. They're going to pass. Their quarterback is in his pocket, their tight end stays in and blocks, and their flanker has come down about 10 yards and is turning in right in front of me. He sees Hank Gremminger coming up from left safety to play him on the inside. He tries to turn out now, and his left foot slips. I see the ball pass his outstretched hands and then I hear the thop-sound it makes as it hits Herb Adderley's hands, and he's got it. He's got it, and he's racing right by me now, down our sideline.

"Bingo! Bingo!" I hear someone, maybe Ray Nitschke,

shouting as the roar starts, and it is our signal to knock down any white-shirt you can reach. I can't see Adderley now or hear a whistle but the play is over.

"Where is it?" I say, and I look at the clock and there is just over a minute remaining.

"About their 18," somebody says.

"Bart?" I'm saying, and then finding him, "Keep it on the ground, and run it in front of the goalposts. Try to waste as much time as you can before the field goal. Let's go."

"Yes, sir," he says.

It was the pass Norb Hecker briefed them on during half-time. That's what it was, and on our sideline they're pounding Adderley on the back now as our offensive team goes in. They go into Brown Right and we run our 65 and Hornung picks up 2 yards off right tackle. From our Red Right, Taylor makes 3 on our 51 off right guard, and I look at the time again. There are thirty-six seconds left and we're right in front of those posts. I signal for a time-out and they call it.

"Okay," I say. "Field-goal team! Be big out there! Let's go!"

Let's hold them out of there now, I'm thinking, and Paul, let's make this one certain. Let's make this one as certain as you ever made anything, because this ball game and this week end—who knows?—maybe this season, young as it still is, has come down to just this one kick. I'm watching Dan Currie, out there on his knees and with a towel in his hands, wiping Hornung's shoe. I hear the whistle and they're lining up. The ball is on the 13, and Starr is kneeling on the 21, and we've got 1.5 seconds from the pass-back to the kick. That's all you need. Hornung has measured his steps now. On that last attempt he was reaching for the ball and hit it too high, and that's why it was short and squirted to the right. Let's plant that left foot straight this time and lock that right ankle and . . .

I see the pass come back and Starr turning the ball as he puts it down. The lines have risen, struggling, and Hornung takes his steps and his foot comes forward. The ball is rising, up over the arms, and it's high enough and absolutely true and goes into the end zone stands. I see the referee's arms fly up in the signal.

I feel empty. After all these years in the game, going back to when I was a kid, I still feel empty, and I look at the scoreboard and it is up there—Visitors 7, Packers 9—and I look at the time and there are thirty-three seconds left.

I should have run one more play, I'm thinking. They may get as many as four plays in here, and I was too hasty and should have waited until fourth down.

They bring Hornung's kickoff back to their 26. On their first pass Willie Davis gets up off the ground to tackle their quarterback as he lets the ball go and its second and 10 and there are seventeen seconds left. They go for the long one to the flanker but he has no chance on it, and there are twelve seconds left.

Won't this game ever end? We put on another good rush and he throws out of bounds across the other sideline. There are four seconds left. Now he's dropping back again. He lets it go to his left halfback on a screen, and we're playing it deep and he has it. He's running to his right now, toward our sideline, and Hank Gremminger is closing in on him. Hank hits him and they go down at my feet. The gun goes off and it's over.

"Wow!" Bill Austin says, and we shake hands.

I'm walking across the field. The crowd starts to come down out of the stands now. The air is filled with noise. I'm looking for the other coach. Finally I spot him and he sees me.

"Congratulations," he says, putting out his hand.

"Thanks," I say, shaking hands. "It was quite a ball game."

"Yes," he says.

Neither of us can think of anything else to say and we part. I walk up the ramp, through the crowd calling to me and into the dressing room with its own noise.

"All right!" I say, raising my voice, and the room quiets down. "That was a great team effort! It was . . ."

I can't go on. My voice has broken and I can feel my eyes filling.

They know me and they know what is happening and they start to cheer. I walk over to Taylor.

"Jimmy," I say, and I shake his hand, "you played a fine game."

"Adderley!" they are hollering. "Adderley!"

"Herb," I say, shaking his hand. "Thank you."

"Adderley!" they are shouting. "Herb!"

"Okay!" I say, raising my voice again. I'm all right now. "Let's remember this. We were the better team. We made mistakes, and let's not forget it. Let's stop making mistakes. Have your fun now. You deserve it, but you get down to work again on Tuesday. That's all."

I walk into the coaches' office and get out of my raincoat

and topcoat and sit down at the desk. Bill Austin hands me a bottle of orange soda and I realize my throat is dry and I start to sip it.

"How about the press?" somebody is calling from the other room. "Should we let them in now?"

"Yes," I say. "Let them in. I forgot."

They come in, a half dozen of them. They gather around the desk, several of them with paper and pencil in hand.

"I thought you'd never get a break," one of them is saying to me. "Two fumbles, two penalties."

"For the record," I say, "Jimmy Taylor had a 101 temperature last night. He played a great first half."

"How about the big play?" somebody says.

"I'd have to say it was the last interception," I say, smiling, because he must be kidding.

"You'd say that interception was the turning point?" Lloyd Larson says, laughing.

"Did the field hurt you?" somebody else says.

"No," I say. "They're a great defensive ball club. You just don't run over them. You don't march up and down that field."

"I think it's safe to say," Larson says, "that if somebody made that third-down pass for you, you'd have something to say."

"I don't think I'll comment on that," I say. "I just think you saw two great squads out there today, and a great ball game."

"But you don't think the field hampered you?" someone else says.

"They both played on the same field," Oliver Kuechle says, and I'm glad he's as tired of that tired question as I am.

"Give their front four credit," I say. "They've got a great front four."

When the press leaves I take off my coach's shoes and white woolen socks. I'm putting on my other socks when I realize I haven't had my shower yet.

"I thought we'd never get out of that ball game," I say to Red Cochran. "That defense of theirs is made up of tigers."

"I don't care if it's all a dream," Red says, beaming. "I just don't want to wake up."

I check the statistics and find that we outgained them in rushing, 129 yards to 107, and in passing, 198 yards to

107, and had 19 first downs to their 12. Bob Houle comes in and wants me to make a radio tape.

"I think you saw two fine football clubs, Bob," I say into the microphone. "We stopped ourselves in the first half and once or twice in the second half, but, of course, we got the big break at the end. I think the people of Green Bay saw one of the finest football games I've ever seen."

Mike Walden asks me to make a tape for him, and I say the same thing again. He asks, then, about the big play.

"Were you surprised," he says, "to see him pass?"

"No comment," I say, "except that he had just completed one with two and a half minutes to go."

I'd like them to remember that, I'm thinking, if they start to get on that quarterback's or my counterpart's neck. Now Tom Miller comes in and says that Bill Howard wants a film for TV, so I go out into the dressing room and under the lights.

"Vince," he says, "it was a great victory."

"It was," I say, "and I think it was one of the finest football games I ever saw."

When we finish it is four-fifteen. A few of the players are still dressing but most of them have gone now and the clubhouse boys are cleaning up. As I walk outside the crowd presses around me, calling my name and thrusting autograph books and programs and bits of paper and pens and pencils at me.

"Just a couple," I say. "I can't handle them all."

"Mr. Lombardi," a man's voice says as I sign a program, "I think if you wanted to you could walk on water."

"Just you, son," I say to a small boy as I take his autograph book and pen. "Then that's all."

I have to force my way through them to my car, and behind me I can hear a group of the other people's fans cheering them as their players come out and get into their bus. I get into my car and manage to close the door.

"Mr. Lombardi?" a small blond girl says, holding a piece of paper and a pencil out to me at the window. "Please, Mr. Lombardi?"

"All right," I say, laughing because she can't be more than about six years old and she looks so worried. "How can I turn you down?"

I'm driving now, down through the parking area and out onto Oneida Avenue. When we have our regular two-minute drill on Thursday, I'm thinking, I'll make it 1:35 instead.

That's all the time we would have had if they hadn't passed and if they had been forced to kick on fourth down. I'll give the ball to our offense on our 20 and I'll say, "All right. It's last Sunday. They're ahead 7 to 6 and we've got one time-out left and there's a minute and thirty-five seconds remaining. Let's go."

Our defense will be even tougher to beat than theirs because they know our plays and they've got their pride, too, and they played a great game today. If the offense takes it down there within field-goal range and Hornung kicks it again it will be just what they need. It will be just what that offense needs because they're feeling now that we had to have that interception to win, and I've got to get them out of that. I've got to make them believers.

I've got to make them believers, I'm thinking, and then the problem all week will be to get them up again, all of them, for next Sunday. After this, how will I ever get them up again for next Sunday?

That's what I'm thinking now, turning off Oneida Avenue in the traffic. Then for the first time I feel the fatigue coming, the tiredness coming all over me.

Green Bay Formations, Plays and Pass Routes

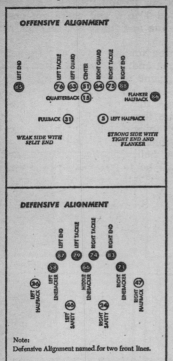

OFFENSIVE ALIGNMENT

LEFT END 85

LEFT TACKLE 76
LEFT GUARD 63
CENTER 51
RIGHT GUARD 54
RIGHT TACKLE 75
RIGHT END 88

QUARTERBACK 15

FLANKER HALFBACK 86

FULLBACK 31

5 LEFT HALFBACK

WEAK SIDE WITH SPLIT END

STRONG SIDE WITH TIGHT END AND FLANKER

DEFENSIVE ALIGNMENT

LEFT END 87
LEFT TACKLE 79
RIGHT TACKLE 74
RIGHT END 83

LEFT LINEBACKER 58
MIDDLE LINEBACKER 66
RIGHT LINEBACKER 71

LEFT HALFBACK 26
RIGHT HALFBACK 47

LEFT SAFETY 46
RIGHT SAFETY 24

Note:
Defensive Alignment named for two front lines.

187

Offensive Formations   Key Running Plays

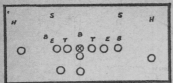

Brown Right against 4-3 Defense

Packer Blue Right 37 against 6-1 Defense

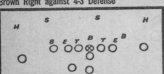

Blue Left against 4-3 Defense

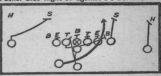

Packer 67 against 6-1 Defense

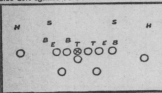

Red Right against Frisco

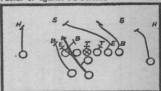

Packer 34X against Frisco Defense

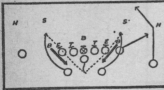

Backs Divide against a Blitz

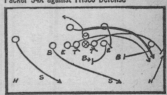

Opponent's Weak Side Sweep against Packer 4-3

188

Some Routes of Packer Receivers

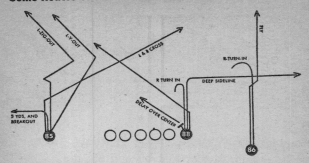

Key Pass Plays

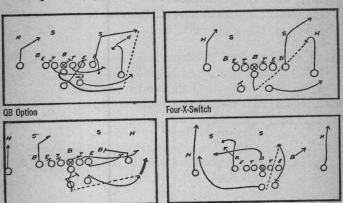

QB Option

Four-X-Switch

Quick Screen

Swing Inside Delay

189

If you enjoyed this book, you will want to read these other absorbing TEMPO BOOKS.

SPORTS

MY GREATEST DAY IN BASEBALL. Thirty-six exciting inside stories told by and about today's top stars and the all-time greats—includes Yastrzemski, Mays, Brock, Ruth, Lonborg, DiMaggio and others.   4879 75¢

DAREDEVILS OF THE SPEEDWAY, by Ross R. Olney. Thrills, chills and spills at the Indianapolis "500"—and the stories of the champion drivers who made racing history.   4877 75¢

WILLIE MAYS, by Arnold Hano (revised edition). Starting from age 3—right through the past season when he hit his 600th home run, this book is the complete story of Willie, his ups and downs.   5337 75¢

THE JOHNNY UNITAS STORY, by Johnny Unitas and Ed Fitzgerald. The amazing personal saga of the sensational quarterback and passing wizard.   4897 75¢

THE MAKING OF A PRO QUARTERBACK, by Ed Richter. From training camp to championship game, this exciting book tells how quarterbacks learn their trade and play the game.   4862 50¢

THE AMAZING METS, by Jerry Mitchell (revised edition). Jerry Mitchell, sportswriter for the NEW YORK POST, tells the truth-is-funnier-than-fiction story of baseball's Cinderella team. The whole wacky, wonderful story of the New York Mets and their cheering, ever-faithful fans. 5340 75¢

PRO FOOTBALL'S HALL OF FAME, by Arthur Daley. The inspiring stories and legendary exploits of Thorpe, Grange, Nevers, Hein, Lambeau and twelve other football immortals. 5313 75¢

WILT CHAMBERLAIN, by George Sullivan. The spectacular career and life story of one of the great basketball players of all time. 4869 60¢

YAZ, by Carl Yastrzemski and Al Hirshberg. Yaz is a home-run hitting, hard-playing champion, with the magnetism distinctive to all of baseball's greats. An exciting saga of a man who may well become a legend. 5330 75¢

SUPERJOE: THE JOE NAMATH STORY, by Larry Bortstein. The thrilling inside story of the man who won the World's Championship for the AFL and the New York Jets—plus an eight-page photo insert. 5316 75¢

GORDIE HOWE, by Stan Fischler. The amazing, inspiring career story of "Mr. Hockey"—Gordie Howe—ice hockey's greatest scorer and most honored player. His career has spanned 21 years of inspired play in the world's fastest sport. 5317 75¢

ADVENTURE

5325. FIRST ON THE MOON 75¢
Hugh Walters. The U.S. rocket Columbus and the Russian rocket Lenin are hurtling toward the moon, each carrying a human passenger intent on making the first landing on its surface.

4871. Rod Serling's TWILIGHT ZONE REVISITED 60¢
Edited by Walter Gibson. By the Emmy Award-winning TV writer, a collection of chilling stories.

Readers will share the terror of a young army officer cursed with the ability to see the glow of death on the faces of men about to die; they will fight under Custer in the battle of the Little Big Horn and marvel at those who miraculously survived—or did they?

5354. MINDS UNLEASHED 95¢
Edited by Groff Conklin. The power and the possibilities of the human mind—as uncharted as deep space—are explored in this collection of science fiction stories by masters of imagination, Isaac Asimov, Robert Heinlein, Arthur C. Clarke, Murray Leinster, Poul Anderson and others expand the limits of the mind and suggest some of the dramatic potentialities of the future.

5356. PLANETS FOR SALE 75¢
A. E. Van Vogt and E. Mayne Hull. In this future world, space travel is a commonplace and business tycoons scramble for advantage on far-flung planets. The action is in the Ridge Stars, a pioneer galaxy as yet uncontrolled by anyone, and the attempts of billionaire Arthur Blord to seize control.

5313. GREAT STORIES OF SPACE TRAVEL 60¢
Groff Conklin. Who knows what strange things will confront those brave Earthlings in the years to come who dare to invade the far reaches of outer space . . . and beyond?

In these stories, a group of science fiction's greatest writers (Isaac Asimov, Ray Bradbury, A. E. Van Vogt, and others) speculate on the nature of those dangers.

5306. ATTACK FROM ATLANTIS 75¢
Lester del Rey. Here is a suspense-filled tale of underwater adventure written by one of America's most honored science fiction writers. In this intriguing tale, Lester del Rey writes of an outcast race that has migrated into the sea and of a young boy who tries to escape from "the city of no return."

5344. VOYAGERS IN TIME 95¢
Edited by Robert Silverberg. A collection of twelve science fiction stories about time travel by such authors as H. G. Wells, Lester del Rey, Poul Anderson and others. Exciting, challenging accounts of voyages back and forward in time—their complexities and hazardous consequences.

4709. MYSTERY OF SATELLITE 7 50¢
Charles Coombs. When Argus 7 mysteriously explodes at an altitude of 42 miles, talk of sabotage runs loud. And suddenly three young people are catapulted from their role of privileged observers to land square in the center of the satellite mystery.

5359. THE WEAPON MAKERS 75¢
A. E. Van Vogt. One of the all-time great science fiction novels by one of the great masters. A psychological suspense novel about a man whose secret is that he is immortal and whose goal is to save the world when the weapon makers forget that they are sworn to preserve peace and attempt to take over the entire universe.